English for Science and Technology

CAMBRIDGE LANGUAGE TEACHING LIBRARY
A series of authoritative books on subjects of central importance for all language teachers.

In this series:

English for Science and Technology

A discourse approach

Louis Trimble

Professor Emeritus
University of Washington, Seattle

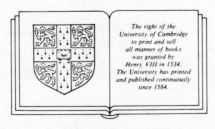

The right of the
University of Cambridge
to print and sell
all manner of books
was granted by
Henry VIII in 1534.
The University has printed
and published continuously
since 1584.

Cambridge University Press
Cambridge
London   New York   New Rochelle
Melbourne   Sydney

Published by the Press Syndicate of the University of Cambridge
The Pitt Building, Trumpington Street, Cambridge CB2 1RP
32 East 57th Street, New York, NY 10022, USA
10 Stamford Road, Oakleigh, Melbourne 3166, Australia

First published 1985

Printed in Great Britain at The Bath Press, Avon

Library of Congress catalogue card number: 85-4210

British Library cataloguing in publication data

Trimble, Louis

English for science and technology: a discourse
approach. – (Cambridge language teaching library)
1. English language – Text-books for foreign
speakers
I. Title
428.2'4'0245   PE1128

ISBN 0 521 25511 2 hard covers
ISBN 0 521 27519 9 paperback

Contents

Contents

Acknowledgements

The author and publishers would like to thank the following for permission to reproduce material:

Cascade Corporation: examples 6.23 and 7.17; John Fluke Manufacturing Co. Inc.: examples 7.11 and 7.12; Harper & Row Inc.: examples 4.4. and 7.19; Honeywell Marine Systems Division Inc.: example 6.9.

1 Introduction

1.1 A bit of background

This book has grown out of research into the characteristics of written scientific and technical English (EST) and out of teaching the findings of this research to non-native students. Although over the years the majority of students have been at university level (primarily engineering and science undergraduates and postgraduates), work has also been carried on with a wider range of non-native learners – from those in vocational training and those at secondary level to those taking pre-university preparation.

We began our study of written EST discourse in 1967 at the University of Washington (Seattle). In this book I use 'we', 'our', 'us', etc. because from the beginning there have been at least two of us working together. Originally, Larry Selinker[1] and I began teaching specialized courses for non-native undergraduate engineering students. We very quickly realized that before we could adequately teach the English of science and technology we had to learn something about it. Our research began with an effort to determine the essential nature of scientific and technical English by finding its major characteristics and where it differed (if it did) from other forms of written English. Initially we brought in two postgraduate students studying for their doctorates: John Lackstrom[2] in linguistics and Robert Vroman[3] in Germanics. Later we were joined by another doctoral candidate in linguistics, Thomas Huckin.[4] The results of our work during this period can be seen from the initial entries in the last section of 'Further reading', pp. 176–8 below.

In 1974 Mary Todd Trimble joined Larry Selinker and me, and after his departure she and I carried on the research and teaching together. The most important shift in emphasis at this time was our moving away from wholly academic EST discourse and applying the rigorous investigative techniques we had developed to occupational English; that is, to materials for a readership ranging from vocational trainees to skilled technicians. From the very beginning of this shift, Mary Todd Trimble was (and remains) the force behind the application of our principles to the several levels at which EST discourse can be researched and taught. The 'we', 'us', 'our', etc. thus refer to those who helped establish our approach to the field and to the still functioning team of Mary Todd Trimble and myself.

In developing the results of our research into teachable classroom materials, we created terms and gave special meanings to already existing ones. For example, insofar as we have been able to determine, Larry Selinker originated the term *EST* to mean 'the written discourse of scientific and technical English'. Before this, we had tried various abbreviated forms, primarily *STE*, but all seemed to call for additional terminology: 'written STE', 'STE discourse', and so on. However, since the term EST became part of the currency of ESL/EFL/ELT, its meaning has broadened until now for many it means 'the field of English for science and technology'; thus it includes oral as well as written discourse.

An example of giving special meanings to already existing terms is the word 'discourse' (already used three times above). Here 'discourse' means a collection of connected language units – such as sentences and paragraphs – that together make up a coherent, cohesive text. We began our work on the assumption that from the point of view of use, language must be studied beyond the level of the isolated sentence. We think, then, in terms of units of text, with the paragraph being the most easily and usefully analyzable such unit.

Thus, when we say that we are presenting a discourse approach to EST, we are taking a short-cut way of saying that we are discussing the teaching of those special characteristics of scientific and technical texts written in English – those characteristics that make scientific and technical English writing different from other forms of written English discourse. A word of caution: 'different' here means 'different in degree' not 'different in kind'.

To sum up, in this book we use the term 'EST' in its earlier sense, as a cover term for the *written* discourse of English for science and technology. Also, we use 'discourse' with the somewhat restricted meaning given it above.

As our research gave us greater insight into the nature of scientific and technical discourse, our teaching changed to take the new information into account. Originally we designed the curriculum for non-native undergraduate engineering students who were advanced both in their use of English and in their subject matter. Later, we broadened the curriculum to include any interested non-native student working in a scientific or technical field. In the last few years of our work at the university, native students taking advanced degrees in teaching English as a second/foreign language (TESL) used our courses as a laboratory. They would sit in on the discussions and workshops and tutor those students who felt the need for special assistance. Each of these changes required us to broaden our research to take the new needs into consideration and to shift our teaching emphasis by broadening this as well.

When we began, we limited our research to what we have called the 'rhetorical techniques' and the three 'rhetorical functions' of *definition*, *classification*, and *description*. As our teaching and research developed, we added the rhetorical functions of instructions and visual–verbal relationships, refined our list of rhetorical techniques, and developed the notion of the 'conceptual' paragraph. Finally, we integrated into our approach the rhetorical – grammatical relationships we found to be most important – and most difficult – for the non-native learner, and we began research on troublesome lexical elements.

There are, of course, several areas of written EST discourse that we have not yet begun to work with. Among these are the rhetoric of introductions and conclusions, and of hypothesizing and argumentation. These and others not mentioned here are clearly fruitful areas for researchers and teachers to work on. Two areas in which research has begun but in which more is needed are treated in chapter 8: 'Tense shifts in the rhetoric of visual–verbal relationships', specifically in the text for a given visual, and tense shifts in the rhetoric of background information. Both of these are important areas of EST discourse, particularly for the more advanced learner.

While these shifts in emphasis had a strong effect on our teaching methodology, they did not alter our basic approach. Early in our work we developed what we call the 'rhetorical approach' to both our research and our teaching. As we refined our research techniques and our teaching methodology, we found more and more support for this approach. Even today we find that in presenting our work at conferences and seminars, in preparing specialist teaching materials, and in furthering our research the rhetorical approach is still a valid and viable instrument. Its continuing use by others in the fields of teaching, materials preparation, and new areas of EST research also indicates that this approach is relevant to today's developing EST needs.

Much of the work described in this book was carried out in the United States, primarily at the University of Washington. The approach, modified as necessary, has also been used in vocational and survival English courses in the United States and has been tested in university, secondary, and vocational classrooms in many countries around the world.

1.2 Some terminology

In addition to 'discourse', I have used another word to which we apply a special meaning: the word 'rhetorical'. This, and its companion 'rhetoric', are defined in chapter 3, along with a detailed examination of the concept 'rhetorical approach'. Here, however, it might be profitable to note that the term 'rhetoric' refers both to organization and to content. 'Rhetoric' is not a substitute for the term 'discourse'; rather it is one part of the concept of discourse. While in our usage both rhetoric and discourse refer to the presentation of information in written (not oral) form, they are not synonymous terms.

1.3   How to use this book

For those who wish to apply this book quickly to their teaching without having to go through the entire text here is a suggested procedure. To get an orientation to the 'rhetorical process', skim through chapters 6 and 7 and then work more slowly through chapter 10. Both chapters 6 and 7 are designed to be used for references and can thus be profitably referred back to whenever necessary. This is especially true of chapter 7. It is somewhat longer than the other chapters in the book because it develops in detail the most essential elements of the rhetorical approach – the rhetorical functions – and is thus the central feature of the book, and also because of the many examples used to illustrate these functions. These examples, along with all the others in the book, serve two purposes: to help clarify the rhetorical points being made; and to provide material that can be used in all types of EST classrooms. Referring back to chapters 6 and 7 will be found an especially useful technique when working through chapter 10, which presents a step-by-step procedure for teaching an EST course.

2 Orientation

2.1 What EST is

The 'Spectrum' (chart 2.1) shows the way in which we conceive EST discourse: it covers that area of written English that extends from the 'peer' writing of scientists and technically oriented professionals to the writing aimed at skilled technicians. In between are shown several of the types of instructional discourse that can be thought of as intermediate between the two extremes.

Peer writing is exemplified by books and articles written by experts in one field for other experts in the same field or for experts in a related field. Skilled technicians are those who differ from engineers in the same field only in that they (sometimes) lack equivalent training in theory. 'Learning texts' and 'Basic instruction' refer primarily to teaching texts although they can include supplementary reading on various levels of difficulty, including journals such as *Scientific American* and do-it-yourself publications for the layman.

A linear spectrum such as this suggests a clear-cut distinction between English for Academic Purposes (EAP) on the one side and English for Occupational Purposes (EOP) on the other. However, a good deal of overlap exists between the two: an electronics engineer and a skilled electronics technician, for example, have a good deal of the same technical language in common and both may rely on the same service manuals for much of their work in the laboratory. At the same time there will be many discourse units they do not share – the engineer will make use of theoretically oriented texts often heavily laced with quite abstruse mathematics, while the technician will have no reason to consult these types of texts. Further, the engineer will read journals that are of interest to him but would not be to most technicians. Similarly, the technician will often deal with manuals of little interest or use to the engineer. Whatever the differences between those operating at either end of the spectrum, neither end is 'better'; each simply represents written EST discourse with some (but hardly all!) different characteristics.

Such differences exist in most scientific and technical fields. One possible perspective on these differences can be seen in chart 2.2, which shows one possible breakdown of academic and occupational fields. The lists shown here are intended to be representative rather than all inclusive. Although 'General English' is set off as quite separate from the other 'kinds' of English, it is, of course, the mainstay of all fields, whatever the purpose for which the language is used.

In sum, EST covers the areas of English written for academic and professional purposes and of English written for occupational (and vocational) purposes, including the often informally written discourse found in trade journals and in scientific and technical materials written for the layman.

CHART 2.1   SPECTRUM OF TYPES OF DISCOURSE

Peer	Learning texts			Basic	Technician
writing	Advanced	Intermediate	Elementary	instruction	writing

CHART 2.2   ONE POSSIBLE BREAKDOWN OF ESP/EST FIELDS

	English for Academic Purposes	*English for Occupational Purposes*
General English	*EST fields*	*EST occupations*
	Engineering	Engineering technicians
	Forestry	Laboratory technicians
	Computer sciences	Mechanics
	Electronics	Electricians
	Mining	Plumbers
	Medicine	Computer operators
	Dietetics	Etc.
	Nursing	
	Etc.	

2.2 Approach

While the approach described in this book was originally developed for particular groups of students in academic environments and our early published research was directed at the EST teacher who is in a university or an institute of technology, the principles presented are applicable to a considerably wider spectrum of non-native learners and to other types of teaching institutions.

Both our subsequent research and the successful application of our approach by teachers faced with students less academically oriented than ours suggested to us that the principles of the rhetorical approach are applicable to a much wider range of users than we had originally envisaged. Later research and application, not only by us but by colleagues in several parts of the world, have shown that by modifying the course design to suit the circumstances (types of students, course purpose, environment, etc.) the concepts presented in this book can be applied not just in courses designed for academic and vocationally oriented EST students but also in those designed for professionals in industry, for journeyman technicians, for technical writers – in fact, for anyone concerned with reading and writing scientific and technical English.

As noted in section 1.3 above, the examples have been chosen for use with more than just the academic student. Only a few of the examples have been taken from highly technical sources; the majority have been chosen to illustrate the entire spectrum of EST discourse. Also, some are not examples of EST *per se* but are about EST. As the later discussion of 'parallelism' (section 4.4) points out, since the purpose of most examples used in the EST classroom is to demonstrate the rhetorical features of EST discourse, those taken from general rather than specific EST discourse are that much more functional in the learning process. The majority of the examples in this book were chosen for just this reason. Further, I have not made 'age' a criterion. The most recently written pieces of discourse are not always those that best illustrate particular rhetorical features; therefore, I have included examples from the 1960s and 1970s and even one from the late 1950s. A comparison of examples will show that the rhetorical features of EST discourse have not changed in the last twenty-odd years.

The students taking a course similar to that outlined in this book are assumed to be fairly advanced in English. Unfortunately, this does not mean that all students are equal in all of the language skills. As teachers we can be faced with students well advanced in, let us say, three of the skills but woefully weak in the fourth: in our experience it is common for students to be fluent in oral production, to have a high level of comprehension in both listening and reading, and yet not be able to write adequately, especially at the level that their scientific and technical studies demand. A similar pattern often exists in respect to the students' technical knowledge. When classes are formed only on the basis of language ability, we can find ourselves with students ranging from rank beginners to experts in their professional fields: we seldom find a truly homogeneous group – either in language or in technical subject matter – in any given class. As a rule we find ourselves working not only with students representing broad ranges of language ability and of technical subject matter but also representing equally broad ranges of personal and subject-matter interests. (It is worth noting here that student interests, for example, hobbies, music, sports, etc., are not always even related to their fields of professional interest.)

In schools that train students for vocational or occupational purposes, a homogeneous class is much more probable: an entire group may, for example, consist of electronic trainees or potential welders. This book, however, assumes that any class the teacher faces will be more heterogeneous than homogeneous in all three areas of language ability, subject-matter knowledge, and personal and subject-matter interest; for this reason, the examples and discussion are oriented toward a 'general' group of students of science and/or of technology rather than those representing any single, specific field of study. (For a detailed discussion of how to work with heterogeneous classes, see especially chapter 4.)

While this book is oriented mainly toward reading skills, it also considers both writing and oral practice. As we will see in the 'Application' sections of the chapters dealing with the basic elements of the rhetorical process (and in more detail in chapter 10), writing can be taught by having the students transfer the strategies developed in analyzing EST discourse from 'reception' to 'production'. We meet this analysis process in chapters 5, 6 and 7, where it is discussed primarily in relation to improving the non-native learner's reading speed and comprehension. It is also treated in chapter 4 when we consider the individualizing process.

Oral production is not discussed directly in this book. However, as a basic step in the rhetorical process is the frequent interchange between teacher and students during the discussion sessions, a good deal of oral work takes place on a non-formal basis. Since the immediate concern of the students during a given class is the material being analyzed and since they are able to identify much of this material as relating to their fields of study (thus giving it a feeling of 'genuineness'), the oral element is, in this environment, authentic. In our experience, the majority of students feel that they are discussing matters similar to those discussed in their technical classes. The result is, then, that we have a 'real' oral situation rather than a contrived one.

2.3 Organization

The body of this book is organized to reflect the patterns of presentation that we devised for our university-level courses. This pattern will be found beginning with chapter 5, which treats the EST paragraph in detail. Chapter 3 provides an overview of our discourse (rhetorical) approach by introducing the basic rhetorical concepts and by defining and exemplifying them in order to orient the reader toward the more detailed presentations later. Chapter 3 also introduces the basic unit of rhetorical analysis, the EST paragraph, and it outlines the rhetorical techniques and the rhetorical functions that play the dominant roles in the analysis process.

The rhetorical techniques are treated in chapter 6 and the rhetorical functions in chapter 7. Since it is the rhetorical functions that play the dominant roles in the analysis process and since each has sub-functions important to the process, in chapter 7 these are treated in greater detail and are exemplified more fully than are the other rhetorical units.

Chapter 8 covers the rhetorical–grammatical relationships that have been found to cause the non-native learner the greatest problems, and which are important to an adequate understanding of the rhetorical techniques and functions. The grammatical features dealt with are the following:
1. Passive-stative distinctions
2. Non-standard use of modals
3. Non-standard and inconsistent uses of the definite article
4. Non-temporal use of tense
5. Relative clauses (treated very briefly)

Chapter 9 looks in some detail at the troublesome lexical elements of sub-technical vocabulary and noun compounds (noun strings).

Chapter 4 is, in a sense, a bridge between the generalizations of chapter 3 and the more detailed treatments of the steps in the rhetorical process found in chapters 5, 6, 7, and 10. The main purpose of chapter 4, however, is to present in some depth the process of individualizing classroom assignments for non-homogeneous groups of students. This presentation includes discussion 1. of the concept of parallelism, 2. of analyzing the types of classes to be dealt with, and 3. of the several types of texts that can be used in developing materials for class use.

Chapter 10, the final chapter, is designed to give a practical orientation to the classroom application of the rhetorical process. It gives a suggested order of presentation of topics and suggests ways in which EST materials are best handled in the class. In addition, the amount of time we plan for each presentation and workshop is noted. Also included are suggestions for group work and pair work in workshop sessions on visual–verbal relationships. Finally, a procedure for controlling student writing assignments is laid out in some detail.

3 The rhetoric of EST discourse

3.1 Introduction

This book examines the rhetorical elements in the discourse of scientific and technical English; it also examines the grammar and lexis related to these rhetorical elements. To many, the terms *rhetoric* and *discourse* are synonymous. However, as noted above in section 1.2, we use the term *rhetoric* to refer to one important part of the broad communicative mode called *discourse*. Rhetoric in this sense we define as follows:

> Rhetoric is the process a writer uses to produce a desired piece of text. This process is basically one of choosing and organizing information for a specific set of purposes and a specific set of readers. An EST text is concerned only with the presentation of facts, hypotheses, and similar types of information. It is not concerned with the forms of written English that editorialize, express emotions or emotionally based argument or are fictional or poetic in nature.

We can further define EST rhetoric by adding that it includes the ways in which information is organized when 'organization' means 1. the sequencing of the items of information in a piece of written discourse and 2. the expression of the kinds of relationships that exist between these items. Also, we can say that EST rhetoric is not concerned with isolated items of information but with the larger discourse units in which these items are found.

As the 'EST rhetorical process chart' (chart 3.1) shows, EST rhetoric exists at several levels in a piece of discourse. Both in our research and in our teaching we have found it convenient to divide the total discourse into the four rhetorical levels shown on the chart.

Level A gives the purpose of the total discourse, this information being usually found in the introductory section of the discourse (in, for example, a technical article). Level B consists of those major pieces of text which, when added together, make up the complete discourse. This level is usually marked in scientific and technical writing by section headings or sub-headings.

The rhetorical process is best seen operating at Levels C and D. Level C is made up of the specific rhetorical functions that are found most commonly in written EST discourse: description, definition, classification, instructions, and visual–verbal relationships between a visual aid and its accompanying text. Most commonly the discourse at this level is presented either in groups of closely related paragraphs or in single paragraphs. A finite number of such paragraphs at Level C add up to one of the sections of Level B.

CHART 3.1   EST RHETORICAL PROCESS CHART

Level	Description of level
A.	The objectives of the total discourse EXAMPLES: 1. Detailing an experiment 2. Making a recommendation 3. Presenting new hypotheses or theory 4. Presenting other types of EST information
B.	The general rhetorical functions that develop the objectives of Level A EXAMPLES: 1. Stating purpose 2. Reporting past research 3. Stating the problem 4. Presenting information on apparatus used in an experiment – a) Description b) Operation 5. Presenting information on experimental procedures
C.	The specific rhetorical functions that develop the general rhetorical functions of Level B EXAMPLES: 1. Description: physical, function, and process 2. Definition 3. Classification 4. Instructions 5. Visual–verbal relationships
D.	The rhetorical techniques that provide relationships within and between the rhetorical units of Level C EXAMPLES: I. Orders 1. Time order 2. Space order 3. Causality and result II. Patterns 1. Causality and result 2. Order of importance 3. Comparison and contrast 4. Analogy 5. Exemplification 6. Illustration

11

Level D consists of one or more of the rhetorical techniques a writer chooses (or is sometimes required to use) as the most functional for presenting the framework into which the items of information given at Level C fit or the most functional for showing the relationships between these items. Frequently, one of the orders and one of the patterns will be found together, thus providing the reader with both a framework and a set of relationships. Although the markers showing the relationships between items of information can consist of paragraphs, as a rule they are found within paragraphs, in single sentences or clauses or phrases.

While the examples listed under each level on the 'Rhetorical process chart' are not exhaustive (particularly at Levels A and B), they do give us an idea of the kinds of information each level contains and how those various units of information relate to one another. For example, if we think of a scientific article – or a chapter in a scientific textbook – that has as its objective the detailing of an experiment (one of the objectives of the total discourse listed at Level A), we find that to achieve this purpose the discourse must include a description of the apparatus being used and a description of how that apparatus works. The writer, then, in developing his ideas is required to choose one or more of the general rhetorical functions listed at Level B in order to satisfy the objective of Level A. In this case, the required function is presenting apparatus used in an experiment: description and operation.

Information on the description and operation of apparatus can only be presented to the reader through the specific rhetorical function of *description* (Level C). Similarly, the use of the rhetorical function of description requires the writer to choose one or more of the rhetorical techniques listed in Level D. By its very nature, discourse concerned with the physical description of an object demands the use of the rhetorical technique of *space order*. And as our sample discourse is also concerned with the way in which the apparatus works, our writer must also choose the rhetorical technique of *process time* and, with it, the relational pattern of causality and result. In sum, the functions chosen at one level almost inevitably determine those to be chosen at the next level down.

Up to this point I have been using the terms 'rhetorical functions' and 'rhetorical techniques' with no attempt to define them or to distinguish them from one another. To clarify how these rhetorical elements work within a piece of total discourse, I define a rhetorical function as a name for what a given unit of the discourse (some finite piece of text) is trying to do and a rhetorical technique as a name either for the frame into which writers fit their information or for the way in which the items of information chosen relate to one another or to the main subject of the given unit of discourse. A rhetorical technique can also show how the informational purpose of one unit of text (at Level C, let us say) relates to the informational purpose of units preceding or following. The rhetorical techniques are discussed in detail in chapter 6.

If the rhetorical function defined above is a 'general' function (Level B), the text covered by this function will be fairly extensive (a section or sub-section) and most frequently will be found under a heading or sub-heading that states the nature of the information that the section or sub-section is contributing to the total communication. If the rhetorical function is a specific one (Level C), then the unit of text will consist of a paragraph (or a series of closely related paragraphs) that contributes to the total communication by providing such information as definitions, descriptions, classifications, etc. The specific rhetorical functions are discussed in chapter 7.

Although it is necessary to discuss all four levels and their relationships to one another when teaching how a piece of discourse is organized (in terms of teaching reading) and how to organize one (in terms of teaching writing), not much class time need be spent on Levels A and B.[1] As noted above, Level A is usually expressed explicitly in the introductory section to a total text and Level B is usually marked by semantically functioning headings or sub-headings. Levels C and D, however, are seldom so explicitly marked; they often require the reader to find clues to grasp the informational purposes of the material. Also, research has shown us that we can best see the characteristics of written EST discourse at these levels (C and D). For these reasons we have concentrated on the specific rhetorical functions (Level C) and the rhetorical techniques (Level D), both in the classroom and in our papers and presentations at conferences and seminars.

For the same reasons, then, in this book we are also concerned primarily with these rhetorical functions and techniques. In addition we look at some of the grammatical areas that present the non-native learner with the greatest difficulties and also look at the special lexical problems inherent in the nature of written EST discourse.

In classroom application, this rhetorical approach has proved itself useful both in teaching reading skills to the non-native student and in teaching the types of writing that both school and professional work in scientific and technical English demand. A large amount of written EST discourse is dense in presentation of ideas, often heavy-footed stylistically, and frequently difficult in terms of grammatical and lexical elements. While we cannot change the style and language habits of past, present, and future generations of writers of EST prose, we can help our students cope with much of it. The rhetorical approach is one way that has, in our experience, proved successful in helping students handle the reading problems of this specialist discourse.

When we turn to teaching students to write scientific and technical English we need to provide additional help. The most persistent problems that we have encountered and their suggested solutions are treated in chapter 10. Here, I only wish to point out that we have found writing best approached as a transfer technique. That is, we have the students consciously practice the rhetorical concepts they have found in their reading by giving them writing exercises designed to make them choose those rhetorical elements most appropriate for a given purpose and a given level of reader. In requiring students to choose specific rhetorical functions and techniques for the presentation of their EST information, we also strengthen their recognition of these functions and techniques when they read EST discourse. In chapter 4, we point out how student reading assignments can lead to directed writing exercises.

3.2 Basic premises

The rhetorical approach to teaching non-native speakers how to read (and secondarily to write) scientific and technical English discourse is built around three main rhetorical concepts: 1. the nature of the EST paragraph; 2. the rhetorical techniques most commonly used in written EST discourse; and 3. the rhetorical functions most frequently found in written EST discourse. Related to these three concepts are the grammatical and lexical elements also prominent in this type of English discourse.

We define this type of written English as follows:

EST writing is that type of discourse that has as its purpose the transmission of information (fact or hypothesis) from writers to readers; therefore it uses only a limited number of rhetorical functions. It does not, for example, make use of such rhetorical functions as editorializing, non-logical argumentation, poetic images, or those functions that create emotions such as laughter, sadness, etc.

With this definition in mind we can now look at the three main rhetorical concepts in the order given above.

3.2.1 The EST paragraph

We define the EST paragraph as follows:

The EST paragraph is a unit of written English discourse that presents the reader with a selected amount of information on a given area of a

subject. This information is so organized by the writer that the
rhetorical concepts chosen and the relationships between these
concepts are the most functional for both the rhetorical purpose of the
paragraph and for the level of reader; that is, the reader's position
in respect to the subject matter under discussion – beginner, expert,
etc.

In working with the discourse of EST we found that the standard definition of 'paragraph' did not fit well with the way that scientific and
technical English is organized and written. The 'standard' definition
contains, as a rule, the following ideas: 'A paragraph is a group of sentences which express a complete thought and which are set off on a page
of text by indentation or spacing.' The difficulty in applying this definition to written EST discourse is that it confuses two quite separate
factors: the first half of the definition deals with concepts ('... a group
of sentences which express *a complete thought* ...') while the second
half deals only with the physical nature ('... *set off on a page by spacing
or indentation*') of the paragraph. Thus, in a sense we have a dual
definition.

The actual organization of a piece of EST discourse is more clearly
seen if we accept that there are two types of paragraphs rather than
insist that there is only one type. These two types we call the *conceptual*
paragraph and the *physical* paragraph. Defining in EST discourse terms,
we say that the conceptual paragraph consists of all the information
chosen by the writer to develop a generalization, whether this is stated
or only implied by the content. The physical paragraph, in contrast,
takes over the second half of the definition above, and so is defined as
that amount of information relating to the generalization which is set
off from other parts of the discourse by spacing or indentation. Here '...
other parts of the discourse' refers either to another physical paragraph
which is part of the same conceptual paragraph or to the previous or
following conceptual paragraphs.

This way of looking at paragraph structure and content also contains
the ideas of 'correspondence' and of 'core generalization'. When a conceptual paragraph is developed by only one physical paragraph, we have
a one-to-one correspondence. When a conceptual paragraph requires
two or more physical paragraphs for its development, we have a one-to-
more-than-one correspondence.

The idea of 'core generalization' is explained as follows. Frequently in
written EST the generalization of a conceptual paragraph is developed
by a rather complex organizational pattern that has the main idea
divided into two or more 'sub-ideas', each represented in the text by a
generalization on a lower level (that is, more specific) than the level of
the main generalization. These lower-level generalizations and their

supporting information are indicated physically as well as semantically by being put in separate physical paragraphs. The rule is: *As long as information – whether it consists of lower-level generalizations or of details at various levels of specificity – is supporting the main generalization, it all belongs to the same conceptual paragraph.*

This concept of 'generalization' is basic to the rhetorical approach to analyzing written EST discourse. We call the main generalization the 'core' or the 'core generalization' when dealing with it in the abstract;[2] we call it the 'core statement' of the paragraph when discussing a concrete example. This concept and that of 'correspondence' are illustrated in examples 3.1A and 3.1B below.

EXAMPLE 3.1A ONE CONCEPTUAL PARAGRAPH COMPOSED OF THREE PHYSICAL PARAGRAPHS (ONE-TO-MORE-THAN-ONE CORRESPONDENCE)

The components composing the urban system can be categorized into two major categories. *These are the land use configuration and the transportation system.* These two categories interact with each other as well as with them*selves.*	Core of conceptual paragraph
Land use refers to the special configuration of supply and demand of opportunities: for instance, the demand for interaction of opportunities is located in institutional, commercial, and industrial areas. The supply side of opportunities is measured in terms of the intensity of attractiveness, which may be expressed by the number of jobs in the specific zone. The spatial location and quantities of these entities (supply and demand of opportunities) in relation to the others are the major attributes of the land use components of the urban system.	Sub-core no. 1
The transportation system determines the ease of interaction between the supply and demand configurations. The transportation system has two attributes. One is the transportation network, which determines the spatial coverage of its service, and the other is the level of service or quality of the transportation system. Both factors have an effect on the interaction between activities.	Sub-core no. 2

EXAMPLE 3.1B   ONE CONCEPTUAL PARAGRAPH COMPOSED OF ONE
PHYSICAL PARAGRAPH (ONE-TO-ONE CORRESPONDENCE)

The transportation system is not the only factor(2) *that influences the level of interaction among various activities,* **though it is a very important one. (1)** *Another factor* **(3)** *is the nature of the activities themselves.* **Assuming that trip productions arise from the residential population and that trip attractions are primarily jobs offered to people, we notice that the qualitative attributes of population and jobs vary widely....**

Core is composed of italicized part of sentence 1, which is embedded between the subject and predicate of sentence 2.

[Source: *The Trend In Engineering*, 22.2 (1970), 29–30]

In example 3.1A the writer has divided his discussion of this particular area of his subject into three physical paragraphs that add up to one conceptual paragraph. The first physical paragraph presents the major generalization, which is the core statement of the conceptual paragraph. The second physical paragraph picks up a key term in the core statement and expands on it, giving the reader the first sub-core. The second sub-core is in the third physical paragraph and is an expansion of the second key term in the core statement in the first physical paragraph. For the core statement to be adequately developed, three physical paragraphs are required. If the writer had put all his information into one physical paragraph, he would have failed to take advantage of the opportunity to use a one-to-more-than-one correspondence to emphasize the importance of each of his two major points (stated as the two sub-cores).

In contrast, in example 3.1B we have a one-to-one correspondence since the core statement is developed in a single paragraph; that is, the physical and conceptual paragraphs are the same and, of course, there are no sub-cores.

This concept of 'core' is of major importance to the understanding of the idea of 'paragraph' in our approach to the analysis of written EST discourse. Occasionally the generalization of a paragraph can be found stated neatly in the first sentence of that paragraph and so equate with the 'topic/thesis sentence' pattern discussed above. Our research, however, makes it quite clear that the generalization of an EST paragraph is not often stated so neatly in a single sentence placed appropriately at the beginning of that paragraph. We frequently find the core statement made up of parts of two or more sentences or consisting of a short phrase buried somewhere near, but not often at, the beginning. At times, the core statement is not found expressed in words but is implied by the nature and organization of the information that makes up the paragraph; that is, the reader is expected to infer the core statement from the context.

Our examples above illustrate types of core statements that are found very often in EST discourse. In example 3.1A the core statement consists of the subject noun phrase (NP) of the first sentence of the initial physical paragraph and of the verb phrase (VP) of the second sentence in the same physical paragraph: 'The components composing the urban system are the land use configuration and the transportation system.' In the verb phrase we find the bases for the sub-cores that begin the second and third physical paragraphs. These sub-cores are stated as second-level generalizations (that is, they are statements which, although still general, are less general than the core – the governing generalization of the entire conceptual paragraph).

The core statement in example 3.1B is more complex than that of example 3.1A. It begins with the subject noun phrase of sentence 2 of the paragraph, goes back up the embedded restrictive relative clause in sentence 1, and then returns to add the verb phrase of sentence 2. The result is 'Another factor that influences the level of interaction among the various activities is the nature of the activities themselves'.

Because of this kind of complexity non-native learners whose exposure to the English paragraph has been through examples of 'topic sentences' placed at the beginning of carefully selected (or made up) paragraphs usually have difficulty in determining the generalizations which govern EST paragraphs.

A more extended discussion of the concept of 'paragraph' as found in EST discourse is given in chapter 5.

3.2.2   Rhetorical techniques

The rhetorical elements that bind together the information in a piece of EST text we call the 'rhetorical techniques'. The most frequently used of these are listed under Level D in the 'Rhetorical process chart', p. 11. All are found frequently enough in EST discourse for us to examine them in some detail.

While the examples listed under Level D in the 'Rhetorical process chart' appear to be discrete items (and sometimes are), actually the concept is somewhat more complicated. First, we are dealing with two quite distinct types of rhetorical techniques: 1. the 'orders' (also called 'natural patterns') that provide a framework for the items of information the writer is presenting, and 2. the 'logical patterns' that indicate the relationships between those items of information.[3]

The natural patterns (orders) are so-called because the nature of the material determines the framework that material is put into. In EST

18

discourse, the most frequent such patterns are 'time order', 'space order', and 'causality and result'. In contrast, the logical patterns are usually deliberately chosen by writers to make clear the relationships between the items of information they have chosen to present to their readers.

Second, the use of one rhetorical technique does not exclude the simultaneous use of others. In fact, it would be very difficult to find an example of one of the orders – time or space – that was not developed in conjunction with one or more of the logical patterns. For example, a paragraph using time order to describe a process requires the use of causality and result. We also find two or more logical patterns working together, with one usually being dominant. We may find a paragraph developed by putting details in their order of importance in such a way that they compare and/or contrast as well.

Several of the examples in chapters 5 and 6 will illustrate these points. Also chapter 5 discusses in detail the rhetorical techniques, which we can also think of as 'patterns of organization'. The discussion includes the criteria for the use of each of the patterns as well as the verbal markers that help the reader identify them.

3.2.3 Rhetorical functions

The rhetorical functions (listed at Level C of the 'Rhetorical process chart') are the foundation of the rhetorical approach to the analysis of written EST discourse. From our research, we have abstracted the five rhetorical functions that occur most frequently in EST texts. These are not treated here and in chapter 6 in any order of importance or frequency of occurrence; however, in both places the rhetoric of description is treated first as it is commonly found not only in isolation but also in conjunction with the other rhetorical functions.

This wide range of occurrence of description is due to the nature of EST material: a large amount of it is concerned with physical structures (physical description), with the purpose of a device and how its parts work (function description), and with processes and procedures (process description).

When we examine types of EST discourse in more detail we will see that, similar to the natural patterns of time and space (rhetorical techniques), certain types of discourse impose certain functions on writers' materials; that is, writers have no choice but to use a specific rhetorical function because the nature of the material requires it. An example is that of discourse written for students new to a field: this kind of discourse demands the frequent use of the rhetorical function of definition since the reader will be faced with new terms and possibly old terms with new meanings.

In chapter 6, the rhetorical functions are treated in detail in the following order:

1. *Description.* This rhetorical function is divided into three types, each of which has distinct characteristics and a clear-cut set of purposes. We call these three types a) physical description, b) function description, and c) process description. Physical description has to do with the physical nature of whatever is being discussed. Function description is concerned with the purpose of some device (usually machinery) and how the parts of that device work separately and with one another and with the whole. Process description deals with processes and procedures and is characterized by the detailing of a series of steps, each but the first usually dependent on the previous step and all aimed at achieving a definite goal. Process description is considered by many to be a special case of function description; however, it is so complex in itself (and is so frequently found in EST discourse) that we choose to treat it as a separate type of the rhetorical function of description.

2. *Definition.* The several types of definition found most commonly in written EST discourse lend themselves well to teaching both reading and writing through the application of the rhetorical approach. The types of definition discussed in this book are a) simple definitions (also called single-sentence definitions), consisting of 1. formal definition, 2. semi-formal definition, and 3. non-formal definition; and b) complex definitions, most of which have special functions such as stipulation, operation, and explication, and which are expansions of simple definitions. This expansion is as a rule in one paragraph, although it can take up an entire text.[4]

3. *Classification.* Classification is also easily divisible into manageable types, thus making the task of analysis easier. We discuss classification from two perspectives: a) the 'direction' in which a classification is made – whether we are finding the members of a given class or are finding a class for one or more given members – and b) whether the classification is explicit or implicit, and if the former whether it is a full or a partial classification. Finally, we discuss the nature of the bases for classification, both those which express similarities and those which express differences.

4. *Instructions.* Instructions are found most often in technical discourse, usually in technical manuals. Instructions can be roughly defined as the rhetoric of telling someone what to do and how to do it to achieve a certain goal. Our detailed investigation of instructions on all levels – from beginners to experts – shows that we can conveniently break this rhetorical function into two major groups: a) 'instructions', the actual telling someone what to do and how to do it, and b) instructional information, that additional information that accompanies most sets of instructions and provides explanations, theory, warnings, etc. We

find instructions themselves to be of two types: 1. direct instructions, which are stated in the imperative, and 2. indirect instructions, which often sound more like suggestions than commands but which actually function as imperative statements. This type of instructions usually contains a modal verb such as 'can', 'may', 'should', and less often 'must'.

5. *Visual–verbal relationships.* This final rhetorical function to be discussed is in some respects more complex than the others. It is that part of what Henry Widdowson has called 'information transfer' that deals with illustrative (graphical) material and the written text which accompanies it. In our meaning of the term, 'visual–verbal relationships' also cover the placement of this textual material (the 'verbal') in relation to the visual – whether the two are separated (and if so what is the precise location of the text) or whether the verbal is part of the visual itself. This placement of text in relation to illustration frequently affects both the kinds and amounts of information the text gives in respect to the illustration and the textual reference to the illustration as well.

As we can see from the 'Rhetorical process chart', these five rhetorical functions are the main ones used by EST writers to develop the general rhetorical functions listed under Level B. In chapters 6 and 7, we demonstrate this relationship more precisely.

Chapter 4 offers our solution to one of the most pressing problems in the teaching of specialized language use: how to cope with a class of students who do not form an even approximately homogeneous group. The typical academic EST class (and most EST classes at whatever tertiary level) is characterized by heterogeneity in respect to the students' fields of interest, to their ability levels in English, to their academic standing (whether undergraduate and which year as undergraduate or whether postgraduate and which degree is being sought), to their subject-matter knowledge, and to their varying abilities with their native language.

Our answer to the above is the application of one kind of individualizing of assignments. In discussing this process in detail in chapter 4 we also suggest a way to determine the make-up of any given class, and we look at a teaching procedure that allows us to apply individualizing more satisfactorily than when we first faced the problem. The term we have devised for this procedure is 'parallelism'.

This way of individualizing assignments is illustrated again in chapter 10.

4 The individualizing process

4.1 Introduction

The approach to teaching the reading of scientific and technical discourse and, to a lesser degree, the writing of it, was originally developed for EST classes in an undergraduate university setting; that is, a wholly academic setting. The students taught were, for the most part, advanced both in English and in their scientific and technical subjects. As the demand for these courses grew, students were admitted with a lower level of English than formerly and, often, with less knowledge of technical and scientific subject matter. Also, postgraduate students requested permission to enter the course that stressed writing over reading. These students were usually well able to read English easily, especially in their subject-matter fields; however, their ability to use language orally and to write it adequately was normally very low. This disparity in student levels – sometimes both in language use and in scientific and technical background – as well as the differing basic subject-matter interests of the students resulted in our developing a procedure for meeting the needs of each individual student as well as we could. This procedure we call the 'individualizing process' or 'individualization'.

Our procedure consists of several steps, as follows. First, we present the rhetorical concept under discussion (that is, the paragraph, or rhetorical techniques, or rhetorical functions) by distributing handouts or examples (sample texts) or, less often, by throwing overhead projector transparencies on a screen. The first set of examples is thoroughly labelled and both the texts and labels are discussed in detail by the teacher. The second set of examples, which are given out as soon as the discussions of the first set are ended, have no labels. ('Label' here means a gloss such as the explanations in the margins of examples 3.1A and 3.1B, pp. 16, 17.) Using this set as a basis for discussion, the teacher now tries to get the students to recognize the points made concerning the first set. Whereas the initial discussions were mostly teacher oriented, these are more evenly divided between teacher and students.

At this point we begin the individualizing process: the students are asked to find *in their own subject-matter reading* examples similar to those in the handouts. Thus, if the nature and structure of the EST paragraph is the subject under discussion, the students might be asked to find examples of paragraphs having a one-to-one correspondence and of those having a one-to-more-than-one correspondence, and to label them as completely as possible. (A bonus to this type of assignment is that often the students' examples are useful for reproduction and distribution for additional discussion or when the time comes for review of this area of the course.) Other types of assignments relating to paragraphs are given in chapter 5.

The individualizing process itself is discussed in this chapter along with the procedures necessary for providing a base for formulating individualized assignments. We discuss 1. class make-up (analysis of students), 2. the technique of parallelism, 3. the several types of texts to consider ('genuine', adapted, synthesized, or created texts), and 4. the individualizing process, using the above discussion points as guidelines.

4.2   Individualization: a definition

Individualization of assignments (that is, the individualizing process) is defined as the process of finding a way to create a set of general assignments that can be used by each of the students in a given class in respect to their individual needs. This type of individualizing makes a *meaningful connection* between what the students have learned in their English classes and what they have learned (or already know about) in their subject-matter classes and/or their fields of interest. This definition does *not* include the meaning that many people have for 'individualizing': the one-to-one procedure; the tutorial. Rather, it refers to a series of specific assignments related in such a way that they all deal with the same area of a subject but are individual within that area and are so designed that they relate to the individual needs of each student.

As we shall see, the individualization process is also a way of making the problem of heavy emphasis on subject matter work for the teacher, the materials writer, or the curriculum designer. However, before we can get to the individualized assignments themselves, we have to perform the following activities:
1. We need to determine the make-up of our class, as this tells us how much individualizing we must plan for.
2. We need to determine the resources available to the students. What books and journals have they access to? Is there photocopy equipment that they can use (and can afford)? Do their class schedules give them time enough to prepare our assignments?
3. What are the students' backgrounds? Have they done much reading and/or writing – in English? in their native language? What is their ability level in their native language?
Finally, we come to the process of preparing for individualized

assignments. This preparation consists of giving the students a solid basis for recognizing – and using – the rhetorical concepts by applying what we have called 'parallelism'.

4.3 Determining class make-up

How an EST teacher proceeds to develop individualized assignments for any given class depends on the factors listed in the preceding section. The first factor, determining class make-up, means finding out just how homogeneous or heterogeneous the class is in terms of the following four fairly broad criteria:
1. The native languages of the students
2. The students' cultural traits related to learning
3. The students' subject areas (or areas of interest, if not the same) –
   a) levels in relation to subject (beginner, intermediate, advanced)
   b) knowledge in subject area or interest area (does not always correlate with level!)
4. Levels of ability in English –
   a) oral production
   b) oral comprehension
   c) reading (in fields of interest and others)
   d) writing (of the types functional to students' work)

A class can be homogeneous in one or more of these areas (for example, all may have the same native language) and still be very heterogeneous. A completely heterogeneous class is difficult to imagine as this would have each student speaking a different native language, have each displaying a totally different set of learning traits, have each studying subjects totally unrelated to the subjects studied by others, etc. Almost as unlikely would be the completely homogeneous class: in absolute terms this must consist of only one student with all the others being that one student's clones.

Often a class that at first glance appears homogeneous turns out to have considerable heterogeneity. An example could be a class of Spanish-speaking students, all in their third year of university, all studying mechanical engineering, all from approximately the same socio-cultural background and, finally, all with much the same ability in English. Yet, a closer look would show that within their field of study there exists a wide range of interests: not all mechanical engineering students have the same, or even similar, technical interests. Some will be interested in motor design, others in refrigeration, others in machine tool design and manufacture, etc.

To face a typical EST class and realize that what we so carefully devised for a previous group is totally unsuitable for the present one can be a disheartening experience. But there is a more cheerful side to the majority of EST classes. Whether they consist of a group of would-be engineers, or natural or physical scientists or a thorough mix, they do share a certain background in common: as students of science and technology they share some knowledge of mathematics and of basic scientific concepts. Most will have been exposed to, and even drilled in, the scientific method. This commonality of background lets us assume a certain amount of homogeneity, enough so that we can take advantage of it in preparing our materials. Nevertheless, we must still face up to the problem of devising some means of overcoming the differences that exist alongside the similarities. Our solution to this problem is the teaching procedure we have labeled parallelism.

4.4 Parallelism

We define parallelism as a process that uses a unit of discourse (in our case written discourse) as a vehicle for carrying the rhetorical, grammatical, and lexical features of EST discourse through the medium of special subject matter. This subject matter is 'special' in that it belongs to no field of study at a level that would exclude any member of a class from understanding it. Thus we can say that the subject matter we work with is always close to a basic level of comprehensibility. Further, this unit of discourse should interest the students without being too dense in content or structure for both their language levels and their subject-matter levels. Finally, the unit should not be so advanced or so esoteric that it gives any student advantage over any others.

Parallelism is successful as a teaching device mainly because of the knowledge that all but the most elementary students of science and technology have in common an understanding of the basic concepts of science and of the scientific method. Also, whatever the fields of study of the students, they will find that the rhetorical techniques and the rhetorical functions dealt with in the discussions and in the examples handed out are the same as those they find in their subject-matter reading. This inevitably gives a feeling of reality to their EST English courses and so helps avoid the charge that these tend to be contrived. As an example, we can choose a unit of discourse that stresses simple formal definition. Once the students understand the kinds and amounts of information a formal definition provides, they have little trouble transferring this knowledge to the more complicated materials they have to read in their scientific and technical courses.[1]

It may be argued that since parallelism is aimed at all the students in any given classroom it is not really individualizing. As we see in section 4.6 below, the result of applying the first stage of the process is that each student has an assignment that is 'specially' designed in relation to individual fields of study.

For examples of parallelism in action we can go back to sub-section 3.2.1 and examples 3.1A and 3.1B. The discourse in these texts is fairly simple in content and in structure and so should not create a comprehension problem for most students at university level. At the same time, it is on a topic that would give advantage only to the most advanced students in the field of urban planning. Thus we can use it with virtually all EST students to illustrate complex core statements and to demonstrate the two types of correspondence and so differentiate between conceptual and physical paragraphs.

The following is a most useful example of a small unit of discourse that can be used to illustrate several of the important rhetorical features of EST texts. At the same time it is simple enough for students at virtually any level: EOP students, beginning academic students, etc.

EXAMPLE 4.1 SAMPLE TEXT CONTAINING SEVERAL RHETORICAL FEATURES

A barometer is a meteorological instrument used for the measurement of atmospheric pressure. Barometers may be classified into two general types, depending on the ways in which they record the pressure of the atmosphere. The mercury barometer is the larger and more accurate of the two types, while the aneroid barometer is more compact but less accurate.

The aneroid barometer is a portable meteorological instrument designed to record changes in atmospheric pressure. It consists of a thin, hermetically-sealed cylindrical metal box, exhausted of air so that the ends of the box tend to approach or recede from one another with change in the pressure of the atmosphere. A train of levers within the box magnifies this movement and records it by an index arm moving over a scale that is graduated to give barometric pressure in feet and inches of mercury.

The mercury barometer is a meteorological instrument used for measuring the pressure of the atmosphere in terms of the height of a column of mercury which exerts an equal pressure. In its simplest form the mercury barometer consists of a vertical glass tube about 80 cm. long, closed at the top and open at the lower end. This lower end is immersed in mercury in a dish. The tube contains no air; rather it contains a vacuum.

[Source: Submitted by a student; precise source unknown.]

[This example has the following rhetorical features:

Paragraph. This text illustrates a one-to-more-than-one correspondence with the three physical paragraphs making up the conceptual paragraph and with the core statement made up of the first sentence of the first physical paragraph plus the names of the two types of barometers from the third sentence of the same paragraph, these names being the bases for the sub-cores in physical paragraphs 2 and 3. (See chapter 5.)

Rhetorical functions. The conceptual paragraph contains three examples of formal definition, a statement of classification, and physical, function and process descriptions. The original has an illustration (not shown here) of the two types of barometers, thus giving us an example of visual–verbal relationships as well. (See chapter 7.)

Rhetorical techniques. The major rhetorical techniques found in this paragraph are 1. causality and result and 2. comparison and contrast. In addition, the second and third physical paragraphs contain space order while the second paragraph (in the statement of process) contains process time order. (See chapter 6.)]

To begin our process we need to choose sample pieces of discourse that parallel the same areas that occur in the students' scientific and technical reading. Once these have been discussed and analyzed, then we can begin to apply the actual process of individualizing. Our initial procedure is to determine which are the best materials to use to present our rhetorical features; that is, we need to choose our 'parallel' texts.

4.5   Types of texts

We find it convenient to divide the written EST discourse that we use for teaching purposes into four categories: 1. 'genuine' materials, 2. adapted materials, 3. synthesized materials, and 4. created materials. Many teachers appear to assume that in teaching EST only 'genuine' materials should be used. However, we have found that the other types are equally useful and for lower (below tertiary) level students often more useful. Since each type has its strengths and weaknesses and is functional in its own particular way, it is useful to look at all four in some detail.

4.5.1   'Genuine' materials

'Genuine' materials are those taken directly from a printed source and presented without alteration. The more homogeneous the group, the more closely these materials should relate to the learners' subject-matter interests.

To make use of 'genuine' materials in the classroom, we need learners with fairly solid backgrounds in English. Guided by this and by the students' basic scientific and technical knowledge, we can choose texts over a wide range of subject-matter difficulty. There are, for example, scientific materials written for absolute beginners in a subject, while at the other end of the spectrum are materials written for those who are experts in the various fields EST students might be studying.

While we can vary the technical level of the subject matter by choosing our texts carefully, we can do little about the language – either the structures or the lexis. The suggestion has been made that to find simple language one should go to children's books on scientific topics. As feasible as this sounds, it seldom works for non-native students. Unfortunately, just because something is written for a child, it is not necessarily (in fact seldom is) presented in language simplified in the way it must be for a large number of non-native readers. Despite numerous efforts, I have yet to find the kind of simplification that is useful to non-native readers in books written for native-speaking children. Writers naturally assume that children have an understanding of many common and basic terms in their own language – terms that are not always included in beginning courses of English for non-native speakers.

A further objection to the use of 'genuine' texts in many situations is that non-native learners who are perfectly capable of grasping the scientific or technical principles involved (they may even have studied them in their own language) still find handling the English lexis difficult. Moreover, they find even more difficult the often complex rhetorical–grammatical features that virtually all native learners understand with little, if any, conscious thought.

Several examples of 'genuine' materials are found in examples 4.2A, 4.2B, and 4.2C, and 4.3 below. In each case it is clear that while each example is in itself useful to illustrate rhetorical features, all pose the same problem: the teacher has no control over the grammatical elements, the lexis, or even the rhetorical features once the choice has been made.

SAMPLE GENUINE MATERIALS

EXAMPLE 4.2A

Holography and photography as methods of forming optical images
Photography basically provides a method of recording two-dimensional irradiance distribution of an image. Generally speaking, each 'scene' consists of a large number of reflecting or radiating points of light. The waves from each of these elementary points all contribute to a complete wave, which we will call the object wave. This complex wave is transformed by the optical lens in such a way that it collapses into an image of the radiating object. It is this image which is recorded on the photographic emulsion.

Holography is quite different. With holography, one records not the optically formed image of the object but the object wave itself.

[Source: Howard M. Smith, *Principles of Holography*, Wiley Interscience (New York: Wiley, 1969), pp. 1–2.]

EXAMPLE 4.2B

Homeostasis

Homeostasis is said to be shown by a (physiological) system if, given a moderate disturbance that tends to displace the system from its normal values, its parts so react and interact that the harmful effects of the disturbance are much diminished.

[Source: Michael A. Arbib, *Brains, Machines, and Mathematics* (New York: McGraw-Hill, Inc., 1964), p. 106.]

EXAMPLE 4.2C

The nature of glass

We are concerned here with glasses, a class of solids that do not crystallize when cooled from a melt and thus do not exhibit long range periodicity of atomic structure. The structure of a glass is often inferred from the analysis of some crystalline modification of the material that forms it.

[Source: R. J. Charles, 'The Nature of Glasses', *Scientific American*, Sept. 1967, p. 126.]

[Example 4.2A is from a book designed for advanced undergraduate engineering and science students. This excerpt is from the Introduction, which is the least technical part of the book. The usefulness of this piece of text lies in its rhetorical features: it gives us a defining statement expanded by description. This description contains a simple definition by synonym. Finally, the two paragraphs provide us with a good example of contrast. The paragraphs are two separate one-to-one correspondences; that is, each is a single physical paragraph making up one conceptual paragraph.

   Grammatically, we have examples of the passive voice and of relative clauses, both of which cause problems for non-native learners. We also have some quite advanced level EST lexis: for example, the way that 'photography' is defined as '. . . the two-dimensional irradiance distribution of an image.' In contrast, much of the lexis is such that any students, non-native or native, should control by the time they reach a level where they would read a book of this nature.

   Example 4.2B is from a book intended for supplementary reading in elementary science courses at university level. This type of book is designed to present a simplified version of a topic. It is not, however, designed for the non-native reader. No concessions are made in respect to lexis or simplification of grammatical structure, as this example illustrates clearly. The most useful rhetorical elements it provides us with are a stipulatory definition (see chapter 7) and an embedded relative clause.

   Example 4.2C is from the American journal *Scientific American*, which has been characterized as providing information for the interested and educated layman. Like the other examples, it makes no concessions – lexically, grammatically, or rhetorically – to its readers. While it is a useful tool to use in EST classes at the university level, it is no less difficult to read than the supposedly more specialized books from which examples 4.2A and B were taken.

Rhetorically, example 4.2C gives us a fairly long and (for the non-native student) difficult formal definition – difficult because of the negatives it contains – and we have a good example of lexis that can confuse all but the very knowledgeable reader: a common non-technical term 'glasses' used in a very technical sense. Because the writer uses the plural, we would normally assume that he refers either to the 'glasses' that improve sight or to the 'glasses' one drinks from. It would take an experienced non-native reader to realize at the beginning of the article that the writer uses 'glasses' to refer to the substance from which all things of 'glass' are made.

To add to the confusion for non-native readers, the writer violates the 'rule' that is found in virtually all textbooks for beginning classes in English, that 'glass' in the general meaning is an uncountable noun. While it is true that students of English are (supposedly) taught early that when an uncountable noun is pluralized it takes on the meaning of 'kinds of . . . .' (kinds of teas, of glasses, of coffees, etc.), this does not seem to stay in the students' minds as well as the 'regular rules' relating to uncountable nouns. Another point of confusion surely must be the writer's use of the uncountable 'glass' with the indefinite article. Again it would take students fairly experienced in reading scientific and technical texts to grasp quickly that 'kind of glass' or 'a piece of glass' is meant here.

Standard references are of little help for the puzzled student since only in scientific and technical dictionaries does the learner find uncountable nouns used in the plural (but not the explanation for this use). The *Longman Dictionary of Contemporary English*, for example, labels 'glass' with the general meaning as 'U'. In contrast, in Godman and Payne's *Longman Dictionary of Scientific Usage* the plural form is given in a discussion of 'polymers and glasses'.]

This type of example text is most useful for students who have shown that they can handle lexis of this difficulty. However, for the majority of non-native readers, it might be safer to leave out examples of this type, as tempting as they are at first look. I am not trying to suggest here that difficult lexis should be avoided simply because it is difficult, (if we set difficulty as a criterion we would be hard put to find any sample materials!) since it is not just difficulty but difficulty *plus* apparent 'rule' violation that tends to create the problems. A good illustration of difficult lexis that has not kept a text from being useful to heterogeneous groups of intermediate level EST students is example 4.3. Few of the students who work with this know the specialized medical vocabulary, nor do they expect to have to learn it. The value for them lies in the rhetorical content: we have easily identified rhetorical functions and rhetorical techniques and an almost classic illustration of a one-to-more-than-one correspondence, with the first of the three physical paragraphs used to state the core and to provide the base words for the sub-cores that begin the following two paragraphs.

EXAMPLE 4.3   A RHETORICALLY USEFUL BUT LEXICALLY DIFFICULT 'GENUINE' TEXT

The autonomic nervous system is separated into two parts, both structurally and functionally. These are called the sympathetic and parasympathetic systems.

In the sympathetic system, the cell bodies of the first motor neurons lie in the thoracic and lumbar portions of the spinal cord. The axions of these neurons exit ventrally from the cord and run to the ganglia lying near the cord, where they synapse with second motor neurons whose cell bodies lie in the ganglia. Thus the synapse between the first and second motor neurons occurs in a ganglion that is at a distance from the target organ, and the axion of the second motor neuron is quite long.

Two principal structural differences distinguish the parasympathetic system from the sympathetic system. First, the cell bodies of the first motor neurons of the parasympathetic system lie in the brain and the sacral region of the spinal cord. Second, the synapses between first and second motor neurons of the parasympathetic system occur in the immediate vicinity of the target organs; the axion of the second motor neuron is thus relatively short.

[Source: Submitted by a student; precise source unknown.]

[In this example the writer gives us a rhetorical function that is often difficult to find: physical description in almost 'pure' form; that is, with virtually no intrusion of function or process description. While in the core statement, we find the word 'functionally' in the phrase 'both structurally and functionally', this conceptual paragraph is clearly an example of development by physical description. The nearest the writer comes to bringing in function description is at the end of the second and third physical paragraphs where causality and result statements tell us that the length of the axion of the second motor neuron is a function of the distance of the synapse between the first and second motor neurons and the target organs. In addition to this example of the rhetorical technique of causality and result, the writer gives us several statements of contrast: The second and third physical paragraphs contrast with one another as a whole and specific statements in

31

physical paragraph two contrast with similar statements in paragraph three.

In terms of the above-described features this is a very useful example, but in our experience it is best limited to classes with comparatively high levels of English. While the rhetorical features are easily identified even by students who have not had a great deal of experience in reading scientific and technical texts, this same inexperience causes them to be put off by the somewhat overwhelming number of unfamiliar words.]

It is obvious that we can use unmodified text materials with fairly advanced students – advanced either in subject-matter knowledge or English or both. However, the fact that we are working with advanced students can lead us into a self-laid trap: so often we find ourselves lured by what seems a perfectly logical idea – gain the students' interest by giving them solid technical material, material they can feel is 'real'. Thus we find ourselves choosing texts for their subject matter rather than for their rhetorical, grammatical, or lexical features. When we begin discussing these features, we find that we are dealing with materials over which we have no control. Our sample text may be strong on technical terminology or scientific method but lack a clear-cut example of whatever rhetorical (or other) point we want to make. Frequently the result is that we either try to compensate by bringing in more texts of the same types (thus compounding the problem) or we try to use the weak example we have and 'talk' it into something more useful, thus taking away any possible feeling that the material is 'real'.

This is not to say that 'genuine' materials are not usable. They can be the best choice, particularly for advanced classes or for those that have the type of homogeneity that can be exploited. However, because of the dangers inherent in 'genuine' materials, they must be most carefully chosen and with the major criterion being functionality: if our immediate topic is the rhetorical function of definition, then we should not choose a text simply because it contains one or more definitions; rather, we should be sure that the chosen text has examples of the kinds of definitions we are concerned with. Do we want to illustrate simple formal, semi-formal, or non-formal definitions? Do we want to illustrate definitions expanded in certain ways?

One way in which we can make use of 'genuine' texts and at the same time make certain that we have the 'right' examples for our immediate needs is to take our 'genuine' materials and give them a modifying treatment. If this treatment is gentle enough, students usually accept such texts as genuine – unless, of course, we just happen to choose one that some of those students are very familiar with. This process of modification we call 'adapting'.

4.5.2   Adapted materials

Adapted materials allow us to stress – and sometimes even create – the features that we want to work with. While the process does not eliminate all of the pitfalls involved in choosing texts because we think (hope?) that they are in the students' fields of interest, we can avoid many problems first, by selecting material as close to what we actually want and need as possible and second, by making minimal changes. Another advantage to this process is that when adapting we are performing teaching-related operations on our selected texts. Thus, involving ourselves in the adapting process can in itself alert us to problems inherent in our particular materials.

However, a word of caution: adapting texts can turn into an awkward and frustrating exercise in preparation if we try to work with too many features at the same time. To try to adapt for rhetorical features (whether the paragraph or rhetorical techniques or rhetorical functions or all of these) and at the same time try to modify grammatical and/or lexical features as well is courting disaster. This is in part because few EST teachers are scientifically trained and so making major changes can result in errors that enable students to recognize a piece of work as contrived. Adapting is more successful – and certainly more of a pleasure – when we make changes in only one area or at most in two areas should these be sufficiently closely related. Examples 4.4 and 4.5A and B below illustrate texts that have been adapted in order to simplify (and to stress) rhetorical features.

Lexical changes are not exemplified here because making such changes is not often rewarding: in scientific and technical discourse there is seldom a precise synonym for a technical or sub-technical word, and even less frequently can we find a simpler (more common) word to do the job being done by the word we want to change. We have done little to the structures except to shorten the original version and to make such changes as help show up the rhetorical elements we wish to point out.

Example 4.4 is the original version. It has been taken from a book designed for American secondary school students planning their future careers. Example 4.5A is an adaptation of the first four paragraphs of example 4.4. The adapting was minimal: physical paragraphs one and two are combined to make a new beginning physical paragraph containing the core of the entire selection (that is, the four-to-one correspondence that adds up to the conceptual paragraph). Paragraph 4 of the original has been broken into two parts to show the separation of the pieces of information that made up the original. The main purpose of this adapting was to provide an example of formal definition expanded by explication (see chapter 7) and to illustrate that breaking a conceptual paragraph into its component physical paragraphs is not purely arbitrary but is done in order to best organize the items of information for the reader.

Example 4.5B is an adaptation of paragraph 5 of the original. Here we have done somewhat more adapting than in the previous example. The first step in this kind of adapting is to take the basic rhetorical feature to be focused on and place it in as prominent a position as is feasible. In our case, this rhetorical feature is the formal definition of engineering. As our purpose is to show a different method of expansion of a definition, we then take the etymological information from the original and use this as a basis for our text. We add to this by inserting a new sentence, which has the purpose of giving the derivation of the term 'engineering'. This not only balances the derivation of 'science' and adds to our expansion by etymology but it also provides a statement giving us an example of the rhetorical technique of comparison and contrast.

While this paragraph (which is an example of one-to-one correspondence) shows more alteration than does 4.5A, we still have made only a minimal number of changes. The result of this rather small amount of adapting provides us with two examples of the development of core statements: 1. two kinds of physical–conceptual paragraph correspondence; 2. two ways of expanding the same definition (by explication and by etymology); 3. several examples of comparison and contrast used to develop ideas within a paragraph; and 4. an example of contrast used to show the relationship of two paragraphs and to act as a transition between those paragraphs.

EXAMPLE 4.4   ORIGINAL VERSION

... we might say that engineering is the process of solving a particular kind of problem (involving the control or utilization of the forces of nature) in a particular way (by the application of principles of sciences, mathematics, and special problem-solving methods) in order to achieve certain practical desired results. More simply, we might define engineering as *the process of harnessing or directing the forces and materials of nature for the use and convenience of man.*

Such a definition of engineering is by no means complete and exhaustive. But for our purposes it is a good working definition because it emphasizes three major points that are critical to our understanding of what engineering is.

First, the word 'process' suggests a continuing activity. Engineering is not a single specific action, but a combination or sequence of actions. It is both an art and a science – a science because it requires specific knowledge, understanding, and use of the laws of nature, and an art because it also requires the human talents of imagination, insight, judgment, and elasticity of thinking.

The words 'harnessing' or 'directing' suggest the how-to-do-it function of engineering. Engineering involves the changing and molding of materials and forces rather than the mere study and observation of them. Finally, the words 'use' and 'convenience' suggest the ultimate goal of engineering: not only to serve the needs of man, but to make things work more easily, more safely, more economically, or more comfortably for him.

We can also see that this simple definition clearly points out the basic difference between science and engineering. The word 'science' is derived from a Latin word meaning 'to know'. The work of science is to expand the boundaries of our knowledge of the laws of nature. The work of engineering is to find useful and practical applications for that expanding treasure of scientific knowledge for the improvement of man's welfare.

[Source: Alan E. Nourse, *So You Want to Be an Engineer* (Harper and Brothers, New York, 1962), pp. 13–14.]

EXAMPLE 4.5A   SIMPLE ADAPTATION

We might define engineering as the process of harnessing or directing the forces and materials of nature for the use and convenience of man. Such a definition is by no means complete and exhaustive, but it is a good working definition because it emphasizes three major points that are critical to an understanding of what engineering is.

First, the word 'process' suggests a continuing activity. Engineering is not a single specific action but a combination or sequence of actions. It is both an art and a science – a science because it requires specific knowledge, understanding, and use of the laws of nature, and an art because it also requires the human talents of imagination, insight, judgment, and elasticity of thinking.

Second, the words 'harnessing' or 'directing' suggest the how-to-do-it function of engineering. Engineering involves the changing and molding of materials and forces rather than the mere study and observation of them.

Finally, the words 'use' and 'convenience' suggest the ultimate goal of engineering: not only to serve the needs of man but to make things work more easily, more safely, more economically, or more comfortably for him.

EXAMPLE 4.5B   MORE COMPLEX ADAPTATION

We might define engineering as the process of harnessing or directing the forces and materials of nature for the use and convenience of man. This simple definition clearly points out the difference between science and engineering. 'Science' is derived from a Latin word meaning 'to know'. 'Engineering' is derived from Latin also, from a root meaning 'to produce'; later it came to mean 'to invent' and 'skill'. The work of science is to expand the boundaries of our knowledge of the laws of nature. The work of

> engineering is to find useful and practical applications for that expanding treasure of scientific knowledge for the improvement of man's welfare.

Adapting in order to make grammatical changes is probably the most frequent (and the simplest) way of modifying texts for classroom use. Example 4.6A is an original text containing a heavy load of passive verb forms and example 4.6B is a partial revision made to show the changes necessary to convert passive forms to active. The revision is only partial so that the passage can be used either as an exercise for the students or as a basis for grammatical discussion.

EXAMPLE 4.6A   ORIGINAL: A HEAVY PASSIVE LOAD

> The d-c relays described in chapter 7 are primarily used with pilot devices to operate the larger contactors or circuit breakers.
> The complete contactor is composed of an operating magnet, which is activated by either switches or relays, fixed contacts, and moving contacts. It may be used to handle the load of an entire bus, or a single circuit or device. However, when heavy currents are to be interrupted, larger contacts must be used. The contacts must snap open or closed to reduce contact arcing and burning. In addition to these precautions, other arc-quenching means are used.

> [Source: Submitted by a student; precise source unknown.]

EXAMPLE 4.6B   PARTIALLY ADAPTED TO ACTIVE VOICE

> We use the d-c relays described in chapter 7 primarily with pilot devices to operate the larger contactors or circuit breakers.
> An operating magnet, fixed contacts, and moving contacts make up the complete contactor. This magnet is activated by either switches or relays. [Complete the paragraph by changing the passive forms – where change is logical – to active forms. Use 'we' when you need a subject for an agentless passive verb converted to an active one.]

Adapting to changes in verb tense, mood or voice is often a quite simple, straightforward substitution procedure. Adapting for other grammatical changes, however, often requires a bit more effort. This is illustrated by the changes made to an original text designed for secondary school students in Yugoslavia (example 4.7A): a substitution of simple past tense for present perfect in order to show a piece of discourse written in an 'historical mode' and several structural shifts made to incorporate relative clauses into the text. Example 4.7B shows the results of these changes.

EXAMPLE 4.7A   ORIGINAL: PRESENT PERFECT TENSE

> The revolution in shipbuilding which began in the 1960s has continued to grow. In order to meet increasing demands for more cargo to be shipped across the oceans, many ships have been reconstructed to carry more and different cargoes – and new ships have been built incorporating changes in size, in ways of handling cargo, in ship design, and in power plants.
>
> This revolution in shipbuilding is best seen in the development of container ships – ships that carry their cargo in large containers, or boxes, to make loading and unloading faster and easier. Much of this new concept in cargo handling has taken place because of technological improvements. Automation has allowed more complex ship designs and greater safety with smaller crews. New alloys and steels as well as new welding processes have permitted ever increasing ship sizes, and new types of power plants – ranging from improved diesels to nuclear power – have contributed to the development of ships up to 500,000 tons, and soon they will be even larger.
>
> [Source: Louis Trimble, Zlata Kipcic, Mia Gottwald, Nevenka Murgic, and Davorka Celmic, *New Horizons: A Reader in Scientific and Technical English* (Zagreb: Skolska Knjiga, 1975), p. 60.]

[The above was written by Mia Gottwald. The book was designed for secondary technical school students in Croatia, Yugoslavia, and was used in several systems there and in other *non-English speaking* environments.]

EXAMPLE 4.7B   ADAPTED: TENSE CHANGED; RELATIVE CLAUSES ADDED

> The revolution in shipbuilding began in the 1960s. In order to meet increasing demands for more cargo to be shipped across the oceans many ships were reconstructed, which enabled them to carry more and different cargoes. Also new ships were built which incorporated changes in size, in ways of handling cargo, in ship design, and in power plants.
>
> This revolution in shipbuilding is best seen in the development of container ships, which are types of ships that carry their cargo in large containers, or boxes, to make loading and unloading faster and easier. Much of this new concept in cargo handling took place because of technological improvements: automation, which allowed more complex ship designs and greater safety with smaller

37

crews; new alloys and steels along with new welding processes, which permitted ever-increasing ship sizes; and new types of power plants – ranging from improved diesels to nuclear power – which contributed to the development of ships up to 500,000 tons. Soon ships will be even larger.

In all adapting, a good rule of thumb is to make the least alteration possible in the sentence structure (unless, of course, the purpose of the modification is to show a different structure) and also make minimal change in the lexis. Even if the lexis should obviously be simplified , it is often best left alone: as I noted above, trying to 'improve' lexis is a frustrating and seldom successful task. A final point: while it may take more time to hunt through several sources for just the right piece of text to adapt, this can reward us, both in ease of adapting and in finding the best material for a given group.

4.5.3 Synthesized and created materials

I lump together synthesized and created materials for purposes of discussion as they are the results of very similar processes. Both give us more control over the grammatical, rhetorical, and lexical features than do adapting or using 'genuine' materials. At the same time, it must be admitted that both synthesizing and creating require more time and effort on the part of the person preparing materials than do either of the other two procedures.

By synthesizing we mean the process of taking 'genuine' materials from two or more sources, deleting the unwanted items and fusing the remaining information into a continuous text. Although synthesizing does not rule out using direct quotations, the fewer used, the more 'real' the synthesized piece will sound: much more control can be achieved by clever paraphrasing than by relying on too much original language. In other words, we can leave the original where appropriate and, when we wish, adapt for specific points of rhetoric, structure, or lexis.

By creating we mean much the same as synthesizing except that our sources are used purely for reference and all of the wording is our own. This method obviously gives us almost complete control in building our units of discourse as we want them, in stressing those grammatical elements we wish to have practiced, and in providing the lexis that is most useful for any given group. Since few of us carry in our heads a body of scientific and technical information that we can produce on call, the procedures involved in creating materials can be very time consuming – especially at the beginning of our 'research'. Even so, the results usually justify this extra time and effort. For, despite the 'genuine materials only' advocates, control over one's material is a vitally important element in teaching an EST class of non-native students, especially those at lower levels. And, clearly, we get the most control from creating or synthesizing.

Example, 4.8 below illustrates synthesizing from several sources, primarily histories of technology and encyclopedias. The purpose of the text is dual: first, to exemplify the rhetoric of description and the rhetorical technique of comparison and contrast, and second to exemplify typical passive-voice technical writing and from this to set up an exercise in a) recognizing the passive and b) learning how to transform it into the active where possible – and logical.

This piece of discourse is relatively short (a little over 200 words) but synthesizing allows us to get in all the features noted above as well as others worth discussing: transitions, demonstratives, and one-to-one correspondence.

EXAMPLE 4.8   A SYNTHESIZED TEXT

One early technological change that had far-reaching effects on man and his environment is that of the plow. Before the late 600s AD the ground was not turned over by plows, but its surface was only scratched, even when the plows were drawn by a pair of oxen. Thus cross-plowing was needed and so fields tended to be made more square. The fairly light soils of the Middle East and the Mediterranean could be worked quite easily by this method, while the heavier soils of northern Europe, on the other hand, could not be. However, by the end of the 7th century (the late 600s), a new kind of plow was being used by northern Europeans. This plow was equipped with a vertical knife with which the furrow was cut; a horizontal piece (which is called the 'share') that cut under the sod; and a moldboard by which the soil was turned. The pressure of the soil against this plow was so great that eight, rather than just two, oxen were required to pull it. Now, because cross-plowing was no longer needed, the shape of fields was changed from square to long and striplike; and because the soil was worked so much more completely, greater harvests were possible.

[The above selection is clearly awkward in using passive forms when active ones would obviously be stylistically better as well as easier to understand. I refer especially to sentence 6, where the 'new' plow is described. Hopefully, the students will change 'with which the furrow was cut' to 'that cut the furrow' and 'which is called the share' to the still passive but simpler 'called the share' and 'by which the soil was turned' to 'that turned the soil'. The other passives sound more 'natural' but most could still stand transforming into actives.]

Example 4.9 is an elementary-level created text, built on the model of example 4.1. Its purpose is to provide an example of parallelism that illustrates the rhetorical functions of definition, classification, and description along with the rhetorical technique of comparison and contrast. Although not specifically designed for the purpose, this text can also be used in a discussion of paragraphing: it has two clear cut cores and one sub-core and it has two separate conceptual paragraphs – the first two illustrating a two-to-one correspondence and the third, a one-to-one correspondence.

EXAMPLE 4.9   A CREATED TEXT

> A thermometer is a measuring instrument used to give the temperature of the surrounding atmosphere. Thermometers may be divided into types according to their means of indicating temperature. The most common types of thermometers are those which use alcohol or mercury inside a glass tube. In fact, we can classify thermometers by the materials they use to record temperatures. Other ways of classifying them are 1) by the type of scale each uses and 2) by their function or purpose.
>
> Four different scales are used for temperature measurement. The Fahrenheit scale divides the temperature between the freezing and boiling points of water into 212 units; that is, degrees. The Celsius scale (often called Centigrade) divides this same range of temperature into 100 degrees. The Kelvin scale begins its measurement at Absolute Zero with its degree intervals (intervals of temperature) corresponding to the Celsius scale – thus the freezing point of water on the Kelvin scale is 273.15°K. The Rankine scale is also an Absolute Zero scale; however, its temperature intervals are based on the Fahrenheit rather than the Celsius scale.
>
> Thermometers may be grouped according to their purpose or function in several ways. One simple grouping is to divide them into a) medical thermometers, b) weather thermometers, and c) scientific thermometers.

I am not suggesting here that we never use 'genuine' materials in our EST work. They do, after all, provide that air of verisimilitude that makes students feel that they are working with something besides materials contrived for the classroom and, therefore, suspect. This reaction is especially true of advanced undergraduate and postgraduate science and engineering students. In fact, a workable rule is, 'The more advanced the class (advanced in both English and subject matter), the more useful are "genuine" materials.' In our experience, the basic criteria for determining whether to use 'genuine' materials or to adapt or synthesize or create them are 1. the language and subject-matter levels of a given group and 2. the features to be stressed in a given teaching sesssion.[2]

The first criterion needs little commentary. Concerning the second criterion, however, it is worthwhile to remember that 'genuine' materials seldom provide us with precisely the features – whether rhetorical, grammatical, or lexical – that we want for any given day. Unfortunately, when they do satisfy these needs, they often include additional (and unwanted) features that tend to distract many students. This is especially true with lower-level groups. We can now add to our 'rule' above: 'The less advanced the class, the less one should use "genuine" materials and the more one should rely on adapting, synthesizing and creating to get the most functional discourse units.'

To return to one of the basic points of this chapter, any of the examples can provide material for parallelism. In our experience, however, the most useful are examples 4.1 and 4.9 for illustrating the rhetorical functions of description, definition, and classification and the rhetorical techniques of causality and result and comparison and contrast; these examples plus example 4.4 for illustrating the conceptual–physical paragraph correspondences and the rhetoric of definition; and examples 4.6 and 4.8 for illustrating the 'passive' style of much scientific and technical writing and for setting up passive–active transformation exercises.

4.6   Individualizing: examples

The following brief discussion makes no attempt to be exhaustive. Detailed individualized assignments are given in each of the chapters concerned with the major topics of this book: the paragraph, the rhetorical techniques, the rhetorical functions, the rhetorical–grammatical relationships, and the problems of lexis. In this section only two examples are given, both based on the assumption that the students are involved in studying the EST paragraph.

Other assumptions on which the individualizing examples are based are the following:
1. The class consists of students with average ability both in English and in subject-matter knowledge.
2. All are undergraduate students, their fields being engineering, premedicine, communications, anthropology, and English as a second foreign language.
3. They have had three sessions on the paragraph. In the first, they were given a labeled set of example paragraphs (examples 3.1A and B), and in the second, an unlabeled set of paragraphs (example 4.5A). The first session stressed the concept of physical–conceptual correspondences and the second that of core statements. In the third, the students were shown a number of paragraphs taken from writings in various fields of science and technology. Some of these examples were untouched;

others were adapted to stress the idea of 'core', the main point of the discussion.

The first sets of individualized assignments were designed to improve reading skills by teaching students to see quickly what a paragraph was going to be about. (The instructions on photocopying and cutting and pasting are not vital to the process. The students can hand copy or type the material if photocopy equipment is not available or if photocopying is too costly. The purpose of photocopying for this type of assignment is to make sure that the students avoid putting their own errors into the material as they so often do when copying by hand.³)

The sample assignment shown in chart 4.1 requires the students to find six different paragraphs taken from their subject-matter reading and is clearly too long to be given as a single assignment: it is a composite of parts of two assignments, one designed to test an understanding of correspondences and the other, recognition of core statements. The instructions following the assignment are also a composite from the two original handouts. Adapting this assignment for class use is discussed in section 10.4, chapter 10.

CHART 4.1   SAMPLE INDIVIDUALIZED READING ASSIGNMENT

Using your assigned books or other reading materials related to your own scientific or technical courses, find examples of the following types of paragraphs:

1. A paragraph with a one-to-one correspondence
2. A paragraph with a one-to-more-than-one correspondence
3. A one-to-one paragraph that has its core statement in the first sentence
4. A one-to-one paragraph that has its core statement anywhere *but* in the first sentence
5. A conceptual paragraph made up of *three* or more physical paragraphs with the core statement in the first sentence
6. A conceptual paragraph made up of *three* or more physical paragraphs with the core statement anywhere *but* in the first sentence

Instructions: Photocopy each example. Trim it and paste it on a sheet of paper that has your name, the course number and the date at the top. Leave space above and below your example. Above each example put a label giving the type of correspondence of that example. Beneath the example give your source *in detail*. On the example itself, *underline the core statement*.

Once the students show that they recognize paragraph types and core statements in their own reading, we can help 'fix' this knowledge by having them write paragraphs similar to those they have already handed in. Chart 4.2 is a sample individualized paragraph writing assignment designed to follow the reading assignments shown in chart 4.1 above.

One way of keeping a certain amount of control over student writing is to have the students take their assignment away and bring back not their completed paragraphs but notes along with a list of sources. They then write their paragraphs in the class from their notes. While this method serves the purpose of the teacher avoiding receiving paragraphs written by the students' native-speaking friends (a not infrequent occurrence in our experience), it still leaves some unsolved problems. First, unless we vet the students' notes, we usually find direct quotes from the source instead of paraphrases. This is often done innocently since many native students have too little control over the language to be able to paraphrase successfully. Second, the method described above requires using considerable class time – a commodity few of us have enough of when teaching. A detailed discussion of this problem of controlling writing assignments, including some suggested solutions, is in chapter 10.

The assignment shown in chapter 4.2 is not the actual one students receive as a handout. In the beginning section only two paragraphs are asked for, while on the actual assignment sheet, the students might be asked for more – depending on the capacity of a given class to do work of this kind. The list of core statements gives only excerpts from the actual lists used. In the complete assignment each field has approximately 8 to 10 sentences for the students to choose from. Also, sentences (topics) are changed according to the fields represented in a particular group.

CHART 4.2   SAMPLE INDIVIDUALIZED WRITING ASSIGNMENT

Choose a sentence from your field and write a paragraph using this as the core statement of a one-to-one correspondence. Do the same with another sentence, using this as the core statement for a one-to-more-than-one correspondence.

Engineering   [This may be broken into several fields.]
1. Statics and dynamics are two basic fields of study for engineers.

Communications
1. Computers that can converse with one another will soon be here.

Anthropology
1. The remains of possibly the earliest form of homo sapiens have been found in East Africa.

English as a second/foreign language
1. There are several basic differences between spoken and written forms of a language.

Additional examples of individualized assignments are given in chapter 10, sections 10.5 through 10.8.

5 The paragraph in EST

5.1 Introduction

In chapters 1 through 4 I have attempted to establish the framework the rhetorical approach to teaching EST fits into. In this sense these chapters are introductory. The remaining chapters discuss the main elements that make up the rhetorical approach, stressing EST reading but also looking at writing. These elements are given in an order that our experience shows is most successful in working with university-level EST classes. However, the presentations do not mirror precisely those of the classroom: how much of a given topic is discussed and how much time is spent on each of the areas (rhetorical, grammatical, or lexical) depends to a great degree on the make-up of the individual class. For example, a group composed mainly of postgraduate students seldom needs as much time to grasp the basic principles of the rhetorical functions as does a heterogeneous class of undergraduates; on the other hand, this group may need considerably more time on the problems involved in writing EST discourse.

The elements that make up the rhetorical approach to teaching EST reading (and, secondarily, writing) are discussed in the following order:

Chapter 5,   The paragraph in EST
Chapter 6,   The rhetorical techniques
Chapter 7,   The rhetorical functions
Chapter 8,   The rhetorical–grammatical relationships
Chapter 9,   The lexical problems
Chapter 10, Teaching the rhetorical process

Each of these topics is discussed in respect to its relation to the total process. Most of the examples are from our university classes. Each example is accompanied by a brief analysis designed so that it can be used as a basis for a classroom presentation of whatever rhetorical element is being illustrated. The discussion of the rhetorical process begins with the paragraph. This should receive quite detailed coverage since the students need a sound grasp of the concepts in order to be able to understand and use the other rhetorical features.

5.2   The EST paragraph

We chose the paragraph as the basic discourse unit for the analysis of written scientific and technical English because it carries information in clearly organized 'packets' and because it shows how the various pieces of that information are related. Also, it separates generalizations from specifics and from one another so that the trained reader can learn to differentiate easily between levels of generality.

To recapitulate, the key elements in the semantic unit of discourse that we call the EST paragraph are the following:

1.   The paragraph is a conceptual concept and it may be realized in a group of sentences (or even in a single sentence) set off from other groups by spacing or indentation, or the demands on the way in which the information is most functionally organized may require two or more such groups of sentences.

2.   The 'conceptual' paragraph is developed around the semantic element that we call the 'core generalization' or, simply, the 'core'. This is the generalization that is supported by the lesser generalizations and/or the specific statements that make up the information in the paragraph. As a rule, this 'core generalization' is the most general statement in the paragraph (but see example 5.1B for the 'exception to the rule'). When we refer to a particular core generalization that is realized in the text, we call it the core 'statement'. While this can usually be put in the form of a single sentence, it is often found as a clause or a phrase or a combination of several parts of different sentences. If our generalization is to be called the 'core statement' of a paragraph, its words must be found somewhere in that paragraph. Otherwise, we have an 'implied' core and we talk about the 'core' or the 'core idea' rather than the 'core statement'. While there is no rule concerning this choice of terminology, we find it more useful for class discussion to be consistent, if only to avoid confusing our students.

An illustration of a generalization that can be stated clearly in a single sentence and of its development in the form of lesser generalizations and specifics (that is, specific in relation to the generalizations that govern them) is example 3.1A (repeated below). In addition to the brief analysis made by the 'notes' in the right-hand margin of the example, we would add the following information to a classroom discussion:

As noted in chapter 3, the core statement is made up of parts of the first two sentences of the first physical paragraph: 'The components composing the urban system are the land use system and the transportation system.' This statement is the broadest generalization in the entire conceptual paragraph (made up, remember, of three physical paragraphs). Lesser generalizations are, in a sense, abstracted from the major generalization to provide the sub-cores for the remaining two physical paragraphs: the first is '*Land use* refers to the spatial configuration. . . .' and the second is '*The transportation system determines.* . . .' We find direct support for our major generalization (our 'core') given by the lesser generalization, 'These two categories interact with each other as well as with themselves.' The other two physical paragraphs then develop our core statement and its supporting generalization.

Each of the two sub-cores is supported by a mixture of lesser generalizations and specific information. An easily seen example is the way in which the sub-core 'Land use refers to . . .' is supported. We have the first lower-level generalization '. . . demand for interaction of opportunities . . .' followed by more specific information: '. . . located in institutional, commercial, and industrial areas.' The second lesser generalization 'The supply side of opportunities. . . .' is supported with even more detailed items of information.

[EXAMPLE 3.1A]   ONE CONCEPTUAL PARAGRAPH COMPOSED OF THREE PHYSICAL PARAGRAPHS (ONE-TO-MORE-THAN-ONE CORRESPONDENCE)

The components composing the urban system can be categorized into two major categories. These *are the land use configuration and the transportation system*. These two categories interact with each other as well as with them*selves*.	Core of conceptual paragraph
Land use refers to the special configuration of supply and demand of opportunities: for instance, the demand for interaction of opportunities is located in institutional, commercial, and industrial areas. The supply side of opportunities is measured in terms of the intensity of attractiveness, which may be expressed by the number of jobs in the specific zone. The spatial location and quantities of these entities (supply and demand of opportunities) in relation to the others are the major attributes of the land use components of the urban system.	Sub-core no. 1
The transportation system determines the ease of interaction between the supply and demand configurations. The transportation system has two attributes. One is the transportation network, which determines the spatial coverage of its service, and the other is the level of service or quality of the transportation system. Both factors have an effect on the interaction between activities.	Sub-core no. 2

Because the idea of 'core' is so basic to the rhetorical analysis of EST paragraphs, I want to look closely at some of the other characteristics of this type of discourse. The first concerns a point we have already touched on – the placement of core statements. The fact that these are not always neat, single sentences handily placed at the beginning of the paragraph can at first cause problems for students (native or non-native) who were introduced to the concept of the paragraph by being given carefully constructed ones with their generalizations made up of the initial sentence. While EST paragraphs do sometimes have their core statements as the first sentence, these are in the minority. Examples 5.1A and 5.1B illustrate these points: example 5.1A has its core statement as the initial sentence ; example 5.1B has its core statement as the second sentence, which is preceded by an even broader generalization than that of the core statement.

EXAMPLE 5.1A   CORE STATEMENT IN FIRST SENTENCE OF PARAGRAPH

> Soil physicists have characterized the drying of a soil in three stages. They are: the wet stage, where the evaporation is solely determined by the meteorological conditions; an intermediate or drying stage, where the soil occurs in the wet stage early in the day, but then dries off because there is not a sufficient amount of water in the soil to meet the evaporation rate; and the dry stage, where evaporation is solely determined by the molecular transfer properties of water within the soil. There is a striking change in the evaporation rate as the soil dries during the transition from the wet stages to the drying stage.

[T. J. Schmigge, 'Measurement of Soil Moisture Utilizing the Diurnal Range of Surface Temperature', *Significant Accomplishments in Science and Technology: Goddard Space Center, 1974* (NASA: Scientific and Technical Information Office, 1975, pp. 2–3. Quoted in Thomas Huckin and Leslie Olsen, 'Teaching the Use of the Article in EST', in Larry Selinker, Elaine Tarone, and Victor Hanzeli (eds.), *English for Academic and Technical Purposes* (Rowley, Mass.: Newbury House, 1981), p. 178.]

This paragraph is an almost classic example of paragraph structure organization of information: the paragraph (an example of a one-to-one correspondence) begins with a one-sentence core statement. This is supported by three statements which, while generalizations in themselves, are specifics in relation to the major generalization. The paragraph is neatly rounded off by a concluding sentence which also relates to the core statement but less directly than the preceding information. The paragraph is also an example of writing for a reader educated in another field of science or technology; it is, in this sense, similar to the level of writing found in the journal *Scientific American*.

As noted above, core statements can be other than the first sentence in a paragraph or the most major generalization of that paragraph. Example 5.1B illustrates both of these points.

EXAMPLE 5.1B   CORE STATEMENT IN SECOND SENTENCE OF PARAGRAPH

> Physical comfort does not depend on temperature alone but on other factors as well. One of the major factors on which comfort depends is humidity. High humidity helps prevent heat loss from the body and makes even high temperatures less bearable. Dehumidifying the air helps the body to lose heat and thus bear higher temperatures. However, beyond certain limits, removing the moisture from the air becomes harmful to the body. The mucous membranes of the nose and throat can become dry, thus increasing susceptibility to respiratory diseases.

[Source: Submitted by a student; precise source unknown.]

That the core statement is the second sentence rather than the first in the above paragraph can best be seen by examining the information given in the supporting information: this information is concerned with humidity, not with the larger topic of physical comfort, of which humidity is one part. The first sentence is obviously the broader generalization and (as is so often the case with initial sentences) is a transition from the preceding piece of text.

Such structures as this can be very confusing to the non-native learner, especially to those who have been taught that the first sentence is the generalization (the thesis/topic sentence) of the paragraph and that all other information in the paragraph supports this generalization. Even when they learn that the subject of the paragraph is not necessarily found in the first sentence, many students continue to have trouble until they are able to differentiate between the several levels of generalization that a paragraph might contain and also between the general and specific information. The ability of students to make such distinctions and at the same time grasp quickly the subject matter of a paragraph is one of the bases for improved reading comprehension and speed and (as explained in detail in chapter 10) for a successful transfer of these reading skills to writing.

Another important characteristic of EST paragraphs is that the majority are deductive in structure. As both examples above illustrate, most EST paragraphs have their core statements near the beginning; that is, the governing generalization precedes most or all of the supporting information.

While this is the structure found in all examples given to this point, it is not the only paragraph form found in EST. Prevelant enough to be worth discussing are three other structures: the inductive paragraph, the 'hybrid' paragraph, and the 'implicit' paragraph. This last is, of course, a misnomer as it is not the paragraph that is implicit but the core statement. Each of these structures is exemplified below.

The inductive paragraph has its core statement found at or near the end; that is, the supporting information precedes the generalization. This type of paragraph is found most often in the kinds of peer writing in which the events (physical or mental or both) leading to a discovery (or new hypothesis, etc.) are given chronologically with the results stated as a kind of climax. A second type of EST discourse in which we can frequently find inductive paragraphs is in a different part of our spectrum – in 'popular' scientific writing as in newspapers and books for 'non-experts'. This type of text is illustrated here in preference to an example of peer writing as it is less technical in vocabulary while at the same time retaining the essential elements of EST discourse.

EXAMPLE 5.2   A PARAGRAPH DEVELOPED INDUCTIVELY

> The first uses of plastics were to replace natural materials such as metal, leather, rubber, and so on. Telephones came to be made of a plastic called 'bakelite'; the soles of shoes and, later, the uppers came to be made of various rubber and leather substitutes; and the Second World War brought about the development of 'butyl rubber' tires and innertubes. Although called 'rubber', things made of butyl were, and are, wholly synthetic. Without plastics we would not have many of the things we take for granted: we would not have several kinds of important electrical insulation nor would we have the wide diversity of photographic film available today. When we look back, we can see *how our lives have been changed by plastics.*

> [The core statement of this synthesized paragraph is in the last sentence. It would not be difficult to make this a 'deductive' paragraph by a simple transfer of the core to the beginning of the paragraph and only the change of one word (e.g., 'If we look back, we can see *how our lives have been changed by plastics.*').]

Both inductive and deductive structures are found in the 'hybrid' paragraph, with specific statements leading to a core and then following from it. Since the core statement is usually in or near the centre of the paragraph, we have a kind of sandwich made up of specific information with the core in between. Example 5.3 illustrates a hybrid paragraph aimed at lower-intermediate-level students.

EXAMPLE 5.3   A 'HYBRID' PARAGRAPH

> Date palms have grown prolifically in both Mesopotamia
> (modern Iraq) and Egypt for many thousands of years. Dates are
> rich in sugar and in such warm climates fermentation into a
> liquid containing alcohol took place fairly quickly. Thus, while
> our first records of *dates being made into wine* come from the
> period *3000 to 2000 B.C.*, we feel certain that it was made *much
> earlier.* Since the fruit itself houses the yeast fungus that causes
> fermentation, making date wine was a fairly simple process.
> The only pieces of equipment needed were a jar to hold the
> date 'must' (the dates and the liquid from them) and a strainer
> used at the end of the fermentation.

> [Source: Adapted from Henry Hodges, *Technology in the Ancient World*
> (New York: Knopf, 1970), pp. 114–15.]

> [The core statement is, as the italics indicate, 'Dates (were)
> made into wine much earlier [than] the period 3000 to 2000
> B.C.']

A final type of paragraph development found commonly enough to be
worth studying is the 'implicit' paragraph; that is, the paragraph
which has its core implied by the nature of the information. In this
type of structure, the writer seems to assume that readers can supply
their own generalizations from the details presented. A paragraph
with an implied core is illustrated by example 5.4, which is from a
peer-level engineering report best used with advanced students.

EXAMPLE 5.4   A PARAGRAPH WITHOUT A STATED CORE

> The spans over the water are made up of triple two-pin steel
> spandrel braced arches with their arch springings situated just
> above water level. The two spans over the land are continuous
> steel deck beams supported by portal type concrete trestles on
> rocker bearings that are located just above the ground level.
> The water spans measure 134 meters between arch pin centres,
> with each of the pins receiving a direct thrust of approximately
> 2,240 tonne. The land spans are 73 meters overall and they
> impose vertical loads of some 1,000 tonne on each of the rocker
> bearings that are under the intermediate support.

> [Source: Extracted by a student from a 'British engineering report'; precise
> source unknown.]

In the following chapters most of the examples are in the form of deductive paragraphs.

5.3   Application

As a rule, we need to give our students several examples of each type of paragraph structure and each type of correspondence to make sure that they have grasped the basic concept of 'paragraph'. We also need to 'fix' this knowledge by having our students make as many analyses as there is time for and, as discussed in chapter 4, by making individualized assignments that require them to find 'real world' examples in their own subject-matter reading. Chart 4.1, p. 42, the 'Sample individualized reading assignment', is a composite of several such assignments designed to be given at the end of the discussion on the EST paragraph.

Among many of the examples brought by the students in fulfilling such assignments we will inevitably find a few that either illustrate our points without needing modification or that could be made to do so with only very minor changes. This, then, is a fruitful source for the kinds of examples we need (assuming permission from the students who have submitted them).

Once we feel that the basic concepts of the paragraph have been understood, then it is time to move to the next stage: the analysis of EST discourse in order to discover the rhetorical techniques. Chapter 6 deals with these rhetorical techniques through the presentation and analysis of 'pre-tested' examples. In discussing how these examples can be used in the classroom, we assume that the students have understood the ideas presented here on the paragraph – just as the teacher must assume that these same students can not only understand the paragraph but can apply their knowledge of it when they begin the more complicated stage of studying the rhetorical techniques.

Here I want to stress the point that learning the rhetorical process is a cumulative activity. We use our knowledge of the EST paragraph to help us analyze for rhetorical techniques. We use our knowledge of the EST paragraph and of the way that rhetorical techniques work to analyze and to understand the rhetorical functions. And we use all three stages of the process to some extent when we work with the rhetorical–grammatical relationships that so often make EST discourse difficult for the non-native learner and when we suggest solutions to the difficult problems created by two of the lexical elements of EST discourse: noun compounding and sub-technical vocabulary. This cumulative aspect of the rhetorical process is shown in chapter 10, beginning with section 10.2.

6 The rhetorical techniques

6.1 Introduction

The rhetorical techniques are those rhetorical elements that bind together the items of information in a piece of EST discourse. These techniques are listed at Level D in the 'Rhetorical process chart', p. 11. While there are many more than we show at Level D, in teaching EST through the rhetorical approach we limit ourselves to just those listed on the chart: the three 'orders' and the six 'patterns', as these are the most commonly found and thus are the most important to an understanding of the relational concepts of EST discourse. Each is discussed with respect to the type of rhetorical technique it represents and to its application in the classroom.

In presenting the rhetorical process we are concerned with the rhetorical techniques as they operate within our basic unit of discourse – the paragraph. In this respect we can think of them as 'cohesive ties' and we define them as the semantic elements, both explicit and implicit, that bind together the items of information within our unit of discourse and, as well, show the relationships of these items to the core idea.

We are also concerned with the rhetorical techniques when they function as cohesive ties between paragraphs; that is, when they operate to show the relationships between the specific rhetorical units at Level C. These ties, in turn, can relate a group of Level C units not just to one another but to the 'purpose' of the group; that is, to one of the general rhetorical functions given for Level B. As noted earlier, however, the rhetoric of Level B is beyond the scope of this book and so in these discussions we limit ourselves to the organizational patterns and relationships we find operating at Level C and, especially, Level D.

In teaching the rhetorical techniques we found that the most successful approach is to have the students equate the techniques with 'patterns of paragraph development'. When the ideas of a given paragraph are tied together by only one pattern – by, let us say, causality and result or process time order – the teaching task is a fairly simple one. Unfortunately, paragraphs are not often constructed so simply: as a rule, we find two or more patterns working together, in which cases we can talk about major and minor patterns of development. A further step is to divide the techniques into the two groups shown in the 'Rhetorical process chart', with the criterion of division being whether the pattern was imposed on the discourse by the nature of the material or by the writer's choice.

Our research into EST discourse shows that the 'natural' patterns (those imposed by the nature of the content) are time order, space order and, at times, causality and result. That the material itself imposes one or more given patterns onto the paragraph does not mean that writers have no options in this regard. They can choose to impose a natural pattern onto the paragraph. In fact, in one sense writers always do this by choosing the particular information they want to make up the discourse.

The other patterns we call 'logical' patterns. These are treated below in the following order: order of importance, causality and result, comparison and contrast, analogy, exemplification, and visual illustration. This order is not intended to show either frequency of occurrence or the importance of the pattern to the discourse, but is arbitrary with the exception that analogy seems to be better understood when juxtaposed with comparison and contrast; otherwise, changes in the order of presentation should have no effect on the teaching process.

The term 'logical' used to describe this set of patterns refers to the logic exercised by the writers when they select one or more as the frame for their material. In the discussion we point out reasons for the writers choosing a particular pattern for a particular kind of information. In chart 6.1 below we indicate the most common semantic markers that writers use to signal each pattern to their readers.

CHART 6.1   PATTERNS OF DEVELOPMENT OF THE EST PARAGRAPH

(Terms following the names of the patterns are some of the markers most commonly found in written EST discourse.)

ORDERS (natural patterns)

Time order
Chronology: dates and clock times
Process: first, second, finally, last, now, then, after

Space order
General: in, out, above, below, to the left, in the centre
Specific: 1 mm directly above, at a 45° angle, normal to

Causality and result
(Both natural and logical patterns use the same terms.) thus, hence, therefore, as a result, causing, so that, such that as, since, as a consequence of

PATTERNS (logical patterns)

Order of importance
first, second, third, most important, least important

Comparison and contrast

Comparison (relates similarities):	in comparison, similarly, in like fashion, as does X, so does Y
Contrast (relates differences):	in contrast, on the other hand, however, nevertheless, by way of difference

Analogy

(Compares things basically dissimilar):	by way of analogy, analogically, by analogy, in much the same fashion

Exemplification
For example, by way of example, for instance, as can be seen

Illustration

(Reference to a visual aid):	as fig. 1 shows, as we can see from Table N, See fig. 3

6.2 Natural patterns

The development of paragraphs by one, or a mixture, of the natural patterns is, with few exceptions, the result of the particular rhetorical function (Level C) that writers choose as the vehicle for their information. If, for example, a mechanical process is being described the writer has no choice but to use process time order since by definition a process is an ordered (in time) procedure with one step following, and usually dependent upon, the preceding step. Similarly, should the physical structure of one of the mechanical elements in this process be described, the writer cannot avoid the use of space order as it is an integral part of the rhetorical function of physical description. Finally, whenever process or function description is the rhetorical feature chosen by the writer, causality and result is found in the text since these types of description require statements of the occurrence of events and of the results of those occurrences.

6.2.1 Time order

Both chronological time and process time are found commonly in written EST discourse, with process time being the more frequent. Chronological time occurs whenever the writer uses a framework of dates, clock times, etc. It is found in historical accounts and in reports of time-controlled experiments. An illustration of a paragraph that has its chronological time framework determined by the nature of the materials is the paragraph (one-to-one correspondence) in example 6.1, which is intermediate level, as are examples 6.2A and B.

EXAMPLE 6.1   TIME ORDER: CHRONOLOGY

> Since the Middle Ages the output and consumption of pit coal had been greater in England than in any other country of Europe. Already during the 13th century, domestic coal consumption in London is said to have been so great that restrictive by-laws became necessary to check the increasing smoke nuisance. During the 17th century, English coal was already shipped to the continent in considerable quantities. The actual 'coal age', however, set in during the second half of the 18th century when it became possible to use steam power for the drainage of collieries, thus permitting the working of deeper galleries under conditions of greater safety.

> [Source: Hans Straub, *A History of Civil Engineering* (Cambridge, Mass.: MIT Press, 1962), p. 165.]

Here the chronological framework is shown by the markers: 'Already during the 13th century'; 'During the 17th century'; and '. . . during the second half of the 18th century'. In addition, we have a statement of contrast, marked by 'however', and, following that, a clear example of causality and result, tied together by 'thus'. The paragraph also contains a more complex set of causality and result statements in the second sentence, where we have a cause (domestic coal consumption) creating a result (increasing smoke nuisance) which, in its turn, becomes a cause creating a second result (restrictive by-laws). The first sentence contains the core statement: 'Output and consumption of coal in England since the Middle Ages (or from the Middle Ages to the late 18th century) . . .' This paragraph, then, can be used profitably as a parallelism device since it illustrates not only a one-to-one correspondence but also three kinds of rhetorical techniques while not using any terms or structures that might be too difficult for intermediate-level students.

Process time is required whenever we have a series of steps leading to a predetermined goal. Examples 6.2A and B show how a particular type of content can require development by process time.

EXAMPLE 6.2A   TIME ORDER: PROCESS (DESCRIPTIVE)

> The first man to produce a practical steam engine was Thomas Savery, an English engineer (1650–1715), who obtained a patent in 1698 for a machine designed to drain water from mines. The

machine contained no moving parts except hand-operated steam valves and automatic check valves, and in principle it worked as follows: Steam was generated in a spherical boiler and then admitted to a separate vessel where it expelled much of the air. The steam valve was then closed and cold water allowed to flow over the vessel, causing the steam to condense and thus creating a partial vacuum. This vacuum pulled water from the area to be drained into the vessel. Then by a further operation of the valves, steam was readmitted to the vessel to force water through a vertical pipe to the discharge elevation.

[Source: J. F. Sandfort *Heat Engines, Science Series S 27* (New York: Doubleday, 1962), p. 11.]

The process time markers are 'then' and juxtaposition of sentences describing the activities that make up the process. Along with the process time we have six instances of causality and result. These are marked either by juxtaposition (for example, 'Steam ... admitted to a separate vessel, where it expelled much of the air') or by lexical indicators: for example, 'causing', 'thus', and 'to' (for 'in order to').

Process time is also found in 'instructional discourse' (as opposed to 'descriptive' discourse). This occurs most often in technical manuals and differs from the standard 'paragraph' structure as the text usually consists of a series of numbered steps, often with a kind of 'shorthand' sentence structure and with the verb in the imperative. While we find the core idea of this type of text most frequently in the heading, we seldom find markers to show causality and result or other indicators of relationships unless our series of steps is augmented by explanatory information. (See chapter 7, section 7.5, for a discussion of instructions.) Process time in instructional discourse form is illustrated in example 6.2B.

EXAMPLE 6.2B   TIME ORDER: PROCESS (INSTRUCTIONAL)

Carriage and Assembly Removal

1. Remove the snap rings from the chain anchors and pull the chain anchors out of the carriage.
2. Secure the carriage with an overhead crane. Remove the carriage by pulling it out the bottom of the mast channels.
3. Remove the two middle and two lower assemblies.
4. Remove the two upper roller assemblies by removing the capscrews that connect the retaining plates to the stub shafts. Pull the roller assemblies off the stub shafts.

[Source: Section 3–4, *Quad Lift Mast Service Manual* (Portland, Oregon: Cascade Corporation, 1974), p. 22.]

The core idea (not a core statement) is given by the heading to the set of instructions. While this material could be put in paragraph form, it would lose much of its value as a set of instructions. The standard procedure is to put instructions in numbered lists with each instruction as brief as is consistent with clarity. However, changing instructions to paragraph form, and vice versa, can give the students useful practice in manipulating verb forms and other structures.

As an illustration, we can take part of example 6.3 and change it to standard paragraph form: 'Carriage and assembly removal is carried out by the following steps. First, we remove the snap rings from the chain anchors. We then pull the anchors out of the carriage. Once the anchors have been removed, we secure the carriage with an overhead crane. We then remove the carriage from the mast by pulling it out the bottom of the mast channels. . . .'

Sentence 1 is the core statement of the paragraph. While it is a 'complete' sentence, it hardly gives us more information than the heading of the original. Nor does using paragraph form help toward achieving the purpose of the instructions. If anything, it can cause a certain amount of interference: it is wordier; finding each step in the process takes more time; and what might be an advantage – the use of relational terms not in the original – is compensated for by the use of numbers and spacing in the original. Disadvantages as well as advantages in sets of instructions are discussed in chapters 7 and 10 along with additional suggested exercises.

6.2.2 Space order

Space order is usually divided, as is time order, into two categories: we speak of 'general' space order and 'specific' space order, depending on how exact the writer is in giving measurements and spatial relationships. In using general space order, writers are merely trying to give us 'rough' pictures of spatial relationships and measurements. In using specific space order, writers are more concerned with giving us precise pictures of these relationships and measurements.

Example 6.3 illustrates general space order. Note that the triode is described with non-precise terms such as 'inside', 'surrounding', 'between', etc. (These and the other 'space' words in the paragraph are italicized.) If readers are interested in knowing just how much distance 'between' represents or how far within is 'inside', etc. then this is not a useful type of space description. If, on the other hand, the readers' interests are in getting only a generalized picture of a triode then the description is adequate.

EXAMPLE 6.3   SPACE ORDER: GENERAL

> We will describe a simple triode as a vacuum tube with three electrodes *inside* an evacuated glass envelope. *Right in the center* will be one electrode, the cathode. It is a specially treated tungsten

wire and is referred to as the filament. This filament resembles the filament in an electric lamp and, like the lamp filament, it becomes white hot when electric current flows through the wire.

Surrounding the cathode and *well spaced from it* is the anode, or plate. The plate is usually in the form of a hollow cylinder, and it collects the electrodes that are supplied by the cathode. *Between* the cathode and the anode, and usually *quite close to* the cathode, is a wire screen or cage that completely surrounds and encloses the cathode. This third electrode is called the grid. Electrons that flow from the cathode to the anode must pass through the holes in the grid.

[Source: Compiled from R. M. Page, *The Origin of Radar*, Science Study Series S26 (New York: Doubleday, 1962), pp. 53–5.]

In contrast, we have specific space order illustrated in example 6.4. The descriptive information in this paragraph is about as precise as any reader could wish. A good test for specificity of space order information is to ask yourself if the object or device being described could be drawn to scale from the verbal description. In the case of example 6.3 this is clearly impossible. Example 6.4, however, is a good basis for a precise visual representation.

EXAMPLE 6.4   SPACE ORDER: SPECIFIC

The Test Section
The test section was constructed of a pure copper cylinder 2 ft 6 in long, 6 in id and 6.25 in od. Both ends of the cylinder were closed with removable Pyrex-glass plates $\frac{1}{4}$ in thick. A fluid port was located at each end of the cylinder.

[Source: A University of Washington (Seattle), College of Engineering Research Report, n.d., n.p.]

[The less common abbreviations used in the above example are the following: id. = 'inner diameter'; od. = 'outer diameter'. These are standard abbreviations used in describing the measurements of any object which has a (roughly) circular cross-section and a tubular (hollow centre) construction. For a discussion of 1) the use of the past tense in this example and 2) the distinction between the passive and stative verbs see chapter 7, section 7.5, and chapter 8, section 8.2.]

6.2.3 Causality and result

Causality and result (often called 'cause and effect') differs from time and space order patterns in that it is seldom found as the major pattern of development of a paragraph. As a rule, we find it helping other patterns, both natural and logical: with the natural patterns of chronological and process time (see examples 6.1 and 6.2A) and with any of the logical patterns, but especially with analogy and exemplification (see example 6.7).

The discussion following example 6.2A pointed out that we find causality and result marked in two ways: by a lexical item or by juxtaposition of information. We also noted a complex instance of causality and result in example 6.1. Outside of the phrase '... became necessary' that example was marked by juxtaposition rather than by any lexical items. The difficulty for non-native readers when faced with this way of expressing relationships between pieces of information is that the only clues are to be found in the logic of the context, and the ability to see this kind of logic is not an easily developed facility. It must be taught. Admittedly, such rhetorical complexity is not too common in EST discourse, but it is common enough to need to be stressed for those students who are reading (or are going to read) difficult scientific and technical English texts.

Some analysts of EST discourse have suggested that conditionality is a separate logical pattern and should be so treated. However, in our experience it is best handled as one type of causality and result. The argument here is that we are dealing with a causal relationship even though it is not yet realized and may not be: if X occurs, then Y will happen.

Few non-native students have any problem in recognizing that 'if' clauses govern possible or potential events. Where many students have trouble is in failing to see that the relationship between the 'if' and 'result' clauses is one of causality and result but contingent on the 'clause of causality' actually occurring. As a rule, once this is pointed out, the concept is quickly understood, especially as the juxtaposition of the clauses makes for a causality and result structure more easily identifiable than many in EST texts.

In terms of teaching, whether causality and result is a natural or a logical pattern is of little importance. That the students can identify the pattern quickly either by noting the markers or by learning to react to the kinds of structures we are concerned with here – these are the important points to be sure of. It is often worthwhile spending extra time on causality and result simply because so many processes and other activities are expressed by scientific and technical discourse that relates actual or hypothetical causes and results.

6.3   Logical patterns

In addition to causality and result the most commonly occurring logical patterns of paragraph development are 1. order of importance, 2. comparison and contrast, 3. analogy, 4. exemplification, and 5. visual illustration. (These are not stated in frequency of occurrence in EST texts nor in any other kind of priority; from early on we used this order and have found no reason to alter it.)

As a rule we find these patterns either mixed with one another (two or more) or in conjunction with time or space orders, but with one more prominent. Which pattern takes on prominence is usually a function of the material that a writer uses in any given unit of text. Very often we can see that a choice of other material or a small change in emphasis or even a different phrasing would result in a different major pattern of development. Thus we might find a paragraph such as that in example 6.5A rewritten so that the original key pattern is changed: instead of the paragraph being developed by 'order of importance', small changes create development by 'exemplification'. In both cases, the secondary pattern is causality and result.

Example 6.5A is an adaptation of a paragraph concerned with 'Exhaust smoke from small engines'; example 6.5B uses the same information but phrases it somewhat differently, thus shifting the emphasis and so the pattern of development.

EXAMPLE 6.5A   LOGICAL PATTERNS: ORDER OF IMPORTANCE

> Research into the causes of smoke in the exhaust systems of small internal combustion engines shows that three factors are primarily responsible for excessive smoke. The most frequent cause is an air mixture that is too rich; that is, the fuel-air ratio is greater than 10:1. The second most frequent cause is oil in the fuel in concentrations greater than 60 cc per gallon of fuel. The result of such heavy concentrations of oil is seen in the dense blue exhaust smoke. A third, and somewhat less frequent, cause is the speed of the engine itself. The lower the speed, the greater the density of smoke from oil burning in the combustion chambers.

> [Source: Adapted from Paul Douglas, *Communication Through Reports* (New York: McGraw Hill, 1957), p. 37.]

EXAMPLE 6.5B   CHANGING THE LOGICAL PATTERN

> 1. *Changing to exemplification*
> Research into the causes of excessive smoke in the exhaust systems of small internal combustion engines shows that there are several factors responsible. For example, one very common cause is an air mixture that has an air-fuel ratio greater than 10:1. Another frequent cause is oil in the fuel in concentrations greater than 60 cc per gallon of fuel. A somewhat less frequent but still important cause is the speed of the engine itself. The lower the

speed, the greater the density of smoke from oil burning in the combustion chambers.

2.   *Changing to causality and result mixed with definition*
Research into excessive smoke in the exhaust systems of small internal combustion engines show three main causes: 1) a too rich air mixture, which means one that has an air-fuel ratio greater than 10:1; 2) a heavy concentration of oil in the fuel, which means one that is greater than 60 cc per gallon of fuel; and 3) slow engine speed, which means. . . .

[This pattern can be presented in several ways. The one above states a common result first and then gives the three main causes that govern this result and provides additional information on each cause by using the phraseology of definition (see chapter 7, section 7.3). We could just as well have begun our paragraph by stating the causes first: 'A too rich air mixture, too much oil in the fuel, and slow engine speed are the three most common causes of. . . .' Making alterations of this nature in a paragraph and then having the students do the same to other paragraphs can provide several fruitful exercises leading to a better understanding of the rhetorical techniques and the ways in which they work to establish frameworks and relationships.]

The following examples of paragraphs developed by the remaining most common logical patterns need little comment as they are all found quite prominently in most types of English factual discourse. However, some observations may serve to point up the elements in the patterns that we find most troublesome to non-native learners. The examples following should not, in themselves, cause problems for the majority of students: they were designed to be used in intermediate-level (and above) classes but have been given quite successfully to students with little exposure to EST English and even less scientific background.

The troublesome elements we refer to are 1. an understanding of the difference between comparison and analogy and 2. grasping the relationships between the verbal and graphic elements of an illustration. We define comparison as 'revealing similarities of things basically alike' and analogy as 'revealing similarities of things basically different'. Quite often we find a paragraph developed by comparison as the major pattern. Analogy, however, cannot stand alone; it needs one or more of the other patterns, logical or natural, to work in conjunction with it.

Visual illustration (graphics) is so called to differentiate it from verbal illustration, which is a special type of exemplification and is not found often enough in EST discourse to warrant discussion. Visual illustration is unique among the patterns discussed in that it requires two distinct parts to form the whole: a text and an illustration. (This topic is also treated from a different point of view in chapter 7, section 7.6, where we take a detailed look at visual–verbal relationships as a rhetorical function. Here, of course, we are looking at the illustration as a technique for relating pieces of information to one another.)

Both scientific and technical discourse rely heavily on graphical material to add information to points made verbally. Illustrations range from the very simple – for example, a drawing of a single line or a circle – to the very complex – such as a set of highly detailed blueprints or circuit diagrams. Unfortunately, the quality of accompanying text does not always match that of the visual element. We find information too skimpy to be of much use to the reader; we find writers forgetting to tell readers where to find the illustration being discussed; and we find information so dense that even an expert can have difficulty with it. While it is not necessary to offer our students a series of 'negative' examples, it is worthwhile to mention (even to illustrate) some of the inadequate writing they are liable to meet in their advanced studies and in their professional careers.

Example 6.9, however, has none of these weaknesses and so is useful with intermediate and, especially, advanced classes. It has an easily read visual, simply laid out, and the text tells the readers what they need to know to be able to relate the visual to the discussion. The lexical element may seem difficult but it seldom causes problems for students who have finished their basic undergraduate engineering courses. Examples 6.6, and 6.8, illustrating comparison and contrast, and exemplification respectively, can also be used successfully with undergraduate engineering or science students. Example 6.7, illustrating analogy, is simpler and is useful even at the secondary level.

EXAMPLE 6.6   LOGICAL PATTERNS: COMPARISON AND
CONTRAST

> Many types of mathematical problems are similar in one way or another as are their methods of solution. However, there are also distinct differences in both types of problems and their methods of solution. For example, many interesting problems in maxima and minima can be solved by elementary methods: that is, by the methods of algebra and plane geometry. But there are many more maxima and minima problems that require the techniques of differential calculus for their solutions. Finally, there are many other problems of a more complicated nature in which quantities are to be maximized or minimized that cannot be handled by the methods of the differential calculus: These require treatment by methods of the calculus of variations.

[Source: M. E. Levenson, *Maxima and Minima* (New York: Macmillan, 1967), p. viii.]

[This example very clearly shows the writer's use of comparison and contrast as the main frame of the paragraph, with the rhetorical technique of exemplification providing the necessary support. Using examples to emphasize the points made in a paragraph developed by one of the other techniques is one of the more common patterns found at all levels of written EST discourse.]

EXAMPLE 6.7   LOGICAL PATTERNS: ANALOGY

Sound waves are created by the compression of the molecules of air, this compression generated by the origin of the sound. The resulting wave motion is analogous to that created in water when a rock is thrown in a pond. By studying the properties exhibited by water waves, we can become familiar with the properties of all wave motion. First, we note that the waves produced on the water by a rock striking it move away at a constant speed: This speed is called the velocity of propagation. Second, we note that the waves have crests and troughs. The distance between successive crests or troughs is called the wavelength. Third, as the waves move past a given point, they cause an up and down motion of the water at this point. This motion is the frequency of the wave.

[Source: Adapted from W. E. Kock, *Sound Waves and Light Waves*, Science Study Series S 40 (New York: Doubleday, 1965), pp. 1–3.]

[The writer marks the pattern of analogy only once, when he uses the term 'analogous' in the second sentence. However, the three times he describes events connected with water waves, he *defines* a term associated with a sound wave. Thus, the readers are presumed to apply the marker and so read 'analogy' each time. In addition to this pattern and the three definitions, we have two instances of causality and result, the first and third 'analogies'. The first is marked only by juxtaposition (a rock striking the water produces waves) and the third by 'cause' (waves moving past a given point cause an up and down motion at this point). It is also interesting to note that the supporting information in this paragraph consists of lower-level generalizations rather than specific statements.]

EXAMPLE 6.8   LOGICAL PATTERNS: EXEMPLIFICATION

Most of the things with which science deals can be measured. Whatever part of nature is being studied, science aims to quantify, it, to express its properties and behavior in terms of measurable quantities. Certain measurable entities can be fully specified by a single number – called a scalar – a number that gives their magnitude or size, telling how many basic units they contain. For example, a length can be fully specified by a single number that represents the number of basic units of length (centimeters or inches or some other such units) it contains; a population can be fully specified by the number of basic units it contains (mice or human beings, etc.) and so forth.

Many measurable entities are not scalars; rather they are vectors. That is, a single number does not suffice to specify fully whatever is being measured; instead, two numbers are needed. For example, traffic flow at Fifth Avenue and Forty-Second Street in New York requires one number to denote the magnitude of flow (say in cars per hour) and a second number to denote the direction of the flow (in, say, degrees, with Fifth Avenue as the baseline). Another example of a measurable entity that is not a scalar is the result of an experiment in which gray male mice are bred with gray female mice, where each of the gray mice is a hybrid of a pure white and a pure black parent. The result of such an experiment cannot be fully specified by a single number but requires an array of numbers arranged according to the skin color trait inherited from each of the parents.

[Source: D. A. Greenberg, *Mathematics for Science Courses* (Amsterdam: W. E. Benjamin, 1965), pp. 163–4.]

[In this example we have a one-to-more-than-one correspondence with two physical paragraphs making up the conceptual paragraph. The core statement of the paragraph comes out of the second sentence of the first physical paragraph: 'Whatever part of nature is being studied, science aims . . . to express its properties in terms of measurable quantities.' The first sub-core follows in sentence 3, where 'scalar' is defined. The second sub-core follows the same pattern, defining 'vector' but using both the first and second sentences of the physical paragraph to present the information. Each of the physical paragraphs uses two examples to support its sub-core. In the first physical paragraph, only the initial example is marked, the second being indicated by the semi-colon following 'contains'. In the second physical paragraph, however, each example is marked separately, the first by the standard term 'For example' and the second by 'Another example of. . . .' Finally, we note that the initial sentence of the first physical paragraph is the largest generalization but, as we have seen before, it is a transition from the previous paragraph and not the core of the one it begins.]

EXAMPLE 6.9   LOGICAL PATTERNS: VISUAL ILLUSTRATION

Vertical Reference Unit

The Vertical Reference Unit (VRU) consists of two single-axis inclinometers, as shown in the figure below. One inclinometer is aligned with the fore-aft axis and the other with the port-starboard axis. The inclinometers operate from a + 15 Vdc source in the System Junction Box. The inclinometers sense the mechanical

angle deviation from the horizontal plane, in the direction of the
aligned axis. The output is an electrical signal proportional to the
mechanical angle.

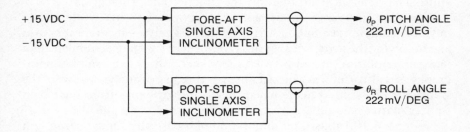

Vertical Reference Unit (VRU) block diagram

[Source: 'RS-7 Digital Acoustic Position Indicator, Operation and Maintenance'
(Honeywell Marine Systems Division, Seattle, Washington, 1976), pp. 4–6.]

6.4   Application

In teaching the rhetorical techniques we can use the same approach as
suggested in chapter 5 for the paragraph: first, handing out paragraphs
annotated to show which rhetorical techniques the writer chose for dealing
with his information and, second, handing out paragraphs without
annotation so that the students can make their own analysis. This second
step can be used for oral work and for testing as well as for in-class
exercises.

   We use two different forms for showing our analysis of a piece of text: one
is to annotate in the margin as in examples 3.1A and B, pp. 16, 17; the other
is to put the analysis in a separate paragraph following the text, somewhat
as in examples 6.7, 6.8, and 6.9 above. From our experience, a successful
way of handling this type of teaching procedure is to incorporate both
forms: we first hand out quite simple examples annotated in the margins
and discuss them, adding information for the students to write into the
margins along with the annotations already there. Our second step is to
hand out paragraphs without annotation but with right margins so that the
students have room to make annotations as they discuss the texts. Up to
this point, all sample paragraphs should be as simple as possible within the
framework of 'good' examples of EST discourse.

   Depending on the make-up of the class, at this point we either continue
the procedure as given below or, should we feel that the students need
more work on the basic concepts of the rhetorical approach up to this
point, we pause to review and/or test. Reviewing is a matter of handing out

examples that illustrate the points that have proved most difficult; testing at this stage is better if kept to those same points: our best results have come from very short tests not designed to test all areas of the rhetorical approach presented so far but only the troublesome problems.

If the class can go on without pausing for review or testing, we then hand out more complex examples, this time with the analyses in paragraph form and following the texts. Because this type of analysis is more complete than margin annotation, it can be used more successfully for complex paragraphs. It is also useful as a model since it is this type of analysis we want the students to be able to make when they bring examples from their own subject-matter reading.

Example 6.10A illustrates annotation of a basically simple paragraph for both the rhetorical techniques and the paragraph elements. Example 6.10B is more difficult and so is analyzed in a paragraph following the text. Since, as noted above, the steps in the rhetorical process are cumulative, this analysis includes comments on both the paragraph – type and core – and the rhetorical techniques.

EXAMPLE 6.10A   PARAGRAPH ANALYSIS: ANNOTATION IN MARGIN

A basic gas turbine engine The basic gas turbine engine consists of three main parts or sections: the air compressor, the combustion chamber, and the turbine. Briefly, here is *how it works:* Air, at atmospheric pressure is pulled into the air compressor where its volume is decreased as the pressure is increased. Since compression of air causes a heat rise the highly compressed air, at high temperature, is forced into the combustion chamber. In the combustion chamber a fuel nozzle (fuel injector) sprays in fuel, under high pressure, to mix with the hot air. The fuel-air mixture is ignited with a resistance type spark plug. As the fuel-air mixture in a turbine engine burns continuously, once ignited the ignition may be turned off. The exhaust leaves the combustion chamber through a duct to enter the turbine unit. Here it delivers most of its energy to the turbine wheel.	One-to-one correspondence. Process time order paragraph *Core statement* *'Since' – causal marker* *'As' – causal marker* *Note that no 'time' words are used. The order of steps is indicated only by the order of events.*

[Source: Adapted from Frederick E. Bricker, *Automobile Guide* (Indianapolis, Indiana: Audel Books, Howard W. Sams, 1972), p. 16.]

EXAMPLE 6.10B   PARAGRAPH ANALYSIS: DISCUSSION FOLLOWS
TEXT

Everything in language depends on order. In writing even a minor
mix-up in the proper ordering of letters and spaces can reduce the
finest phrase to gibberish. To achieve this proper order in written
language, we must first agree on an alphabet and adopt
conventions on the ordering of letters (proper spelling) to form
words. Secondly, we must assign proper meanings to words,
individually and in context. Thirdly, we must accept rules of
grammar establishing the order of words in phrases and sentences,
these rules reflecting, of course, the natural use of the language as
developed over time, not the artificial uses prescribed by the so-
called purists. And, fourthly, we must develop and obey laws of
logic in the association of the ideas expressed by words, phrases,
sentences, and paragraphs. If we violate these rules, we disrupt –
even destroy – the communication of thought.

[Source: Adapted from D. G. Fink, *Computers and the Human Mind*, Science
Study Series S 43 (New York: Doubleday, 1966), p. 61.]

Analysis of paragraph
[Since this paragraph is structured as a series of steps toward a
definite goal, we have an example of a time process paragraph, even
though we are not concerned with a mechanical object as in our
previous time process paragraphs. The core generalization is not
stated completely but is an expansion of the first half of sentence 3,
giving us, 'To achieve order in written language we must follow these
rules.' The first sentence is the largest generalization in the paragraph
but it does not govern the information that follows: it is a transition
from the previous paragraph. The second sentence is a lesser
generalization that works backward to expand on the initial sentence
and forward to set up the topic 'written language', which we find first
used in the third sentence. This sentence is a generalization on the
same level as the second sentence and it specifies the topic, equating
'writing' (in sentence two) with 'written language'. In the final
sentence we have conditionality; that is, potential cause and result.]

The levels of language and subject-matter difficulty of the paragraphs
above, and for most of the examples up to this point in the book, are low
enough to be usable with any tertiary-level EST class. For very homogeneous groups, of course, examples more closely related to their field of
study would be more appropriate.

All of these examples have been used with university-level students
ranging from first-year undergraduates in arts and social sciences to
science and technology students at all levels from beginners to doctoral
candidates. Since the purpose of the class work is to teach students to use
the rhetorical process as a tool for analyzing written EST discourse,

whether the subject matter is more historical or more currently technical seems to be of little importance at this stage. What we find important is that the examples chosen work well in the 'parallelism' process by stressing the particularly rhetorical elements we are teaching and not being too cluttered with other elements that can be distracting. Of course, what is meant by 'too cluttered' changes as we work with the rhetorical approach: by the time the students finish the three stages of the process (the paragraph, the rhetorical techniques, and the rhetorical functions), few paragraphs can be said to be 'too cluttered' since all of the rhetorical elements will have been taught.

Further application of the rhetorical process at this point follows the pattern laid down in the discussion of individualized assignments. Now we can expand those assignments, having our students find one or more rhetorical techniques and a specific paragraph type together. The chart in chapter 10, section 10.5, illustrates a small sample of possible assignments asking for the rhetorical techniques alone or in conjunction with types of correspondences and cores.

The danger in making individualized assignments is in our asking too much of the students at one time. If we give assignments requiring, let us say, a half dozen different paragraphs – each to have an analysis – we must be sure that the students have time enough to do a proper job. A painful lesson most of us learn early in teaching EST is that science and technology students are more interested in their subject-matter courses than in their English courses. The result is that, when they are pressed for time, the English course is the one sacrificed first. Nevertheless, if we tailor our assignments by having the students find the sample paragraphs but not make analyses, we are losing a good opportunity to find out how much each student really understands about the rhetorical process (especially if we have the analyses written in class) and also losing an opportunity to work on student writing.

The application of the rhetorical process is discussed at the end of chapters 7, 8 and 9 and in more detail in chapter 10.

7 The rhetorical functions

7.1 Introduction

As I noted in chapter 3, the rhetorical functions are the heart of the rhetorical process presented in this book. In a sense the preceding chapters have laid the groundwork for this and the following two chapters (chapters 7, 8, and 9). These, in turn, provide the major bases for the procedures that allow the students to discover which lexical, grammatical and rhetorical features writers have chosen to best present their information. We feel that by teaching readers to make these discoveries in a systemic manner, they are able to understand more clearly the concepts involved in a writer's organization (that is, the writer's rhetoric) and so relate the ideas in the discourse more quickly and easily to similar concepts.

The successful application of this discovery procedure is based on three assumptions:
1. The basic rhetorical functions found commonly in EST discourse are fundamental parts of the organization of scientific and technical information.
2. These rhetorical functions and their related grammatical elements are capable of being isolated and studied separately as well as in the total context of a piece of discourse.
3. Each rhetorical function provides readers with different kinds and different amounts of information. As a result, each function is clearly separable and identifiable. (This assumption is the most important of the three for the person applying the procedure.)

In sum, the discovery procedure assumes that the basic rhetorical functions treated here are fundamental elements in the organization of a piece of text and that they are also intimately related to certain grammatical and lexical elements. Therefore, a clear recognition and understanding of all three of these elements as well as of the paragraph and the rhetorical techniques is necessary for full comprehension of written EST discourse.

The discovery procedure is carried out in five steps which, while distinct, are interdependent:
Step 1. The determination of the core generalization and the structure (correspondence) of the discourse unit (in our case, the paragraph) that is being analyzed. This enables readers to know what

specific subject this piece of discourse is dealing with. It also guides them in separating general from specific concepts and in understanding different levels of generality. (Chapter 5)

Step 2. The determination of the rhetorical techniques chosen by the writer. The readers can now see the organizational framework of the discourse unit being analyzed, the relationships that exist between the items of information within this framework, and the relationships between the units that make up the total discourse. (Chapter 6)

Step 3. The determination of the specific rhetorical function (or functions) that writers have chosen (or which their material required them to use) for presenting their major items of information. This, added to the information gained from steps 1 and 2 above, enables the reader to see the total organizational (rhetorical) pattern of the unit of discourse. (Chapter 7)

Step 4. The determination of the rhetorical–grammatical relationships; that is, of the specific grammatical elements which appear to be governed by the rhetorical functions that writers choose to carry their information. This helps readers understand why a particular piece of grammar (for example, a verb tense or mood or definite article) is used in a particular text when this use may seem to violate the logic or the 'rules' of the language. (Chapter 8)

Step 5. The determination of the lexical items that most often confuse readers. This enables readers to get the full meaning from a piece of text and thus, in conjunction with the other steps in the procedure, provides a more complete understanding of the unit of discourse being analyzed. (Chapter 9)

In this chapter we work our way through the application of step 3: the determination of the rhetorical functions writers choose. These functions (Level C of the 'Rhetorical process chart') are discussed in respect to the kinds and amounts of information each provides the reader. The functions and their 'sub-functions' are outlined here in the order treated below:

1. Description – physical, function, and process description
2. Definition – formal, semi-formal, non-formal, and expanded definition
3. Classification – complete and partial classification
4. Instructions – direct instructions, indirect instructions, and· instructional information
5. Visual–verbal relationships – text information, text placement, and placement of visuals

7.2   The rhetoric of description

In our research into the nature of written EST discourse we isolated three major types of descriptive information: physical description, function description, and process description. These are not mutually exclusive: for example, we often find a text developed mainly by physical description containing some function description and a text developed mainly by function or process description containing some physical description. From each of these types of description the reader gets a different kind and amount of information.

7.2.1   Physical description

Physical description gives the physical characteristics of an object and the spatial relations of the parts of the object to one another and to the whole, and of the whole to other objects concerned, if any. The physical characteristics most frequently described are dimension, shape, weight, material, volume, colour, and texture. (This list does not imply any order of importance or frequency of occurrence.)

Physical descriptions are found in EST discourse ranging from the very general to the very specific. General physical description uses such locative terms as 'above', 'below', 'in the center', 'to the right', 'at an angle to', 'near', etc. In contrast, specific physical description requires much more precise terms: '1 mm directly above', 'at an angle of 45°', '2 cm out from the perimeter', etc.

Since the rhetorical function of physical description and the rhetorical technique (pattern of development) of space order are clearly tied together, the examples illustrating general and specific space order (chapter 6, examples 6.3 and 6.4) also illustrate general and specific physical description. The difference between the rhetorical technique of space order and the rhetorical function of physical description is that physical description refers to the purpose of a piece of discourse while space order refers to the relational framework into which writers fit their material. Thus, in space order terms, in the examples in chapter 6, the material consists of the important (to the writer) physical characteristics of the objects being described; in physical description terms, the purpose of the paragraphs is to describe the objects physically – in general terms in example 6.3 and in specific terms in example 6.4. Other examples of space order are found in the examples illustrating function and process descriptions, and also in chapter 10.

7.2.2   Function description

Function description gives the reader information relating, as a rule, to a device of some kind. This information falls into two broad categories:

71

The rhetorical functions

1. the use or purpose of the device (for example, 'The helical gear reduces the ratio. . . .'); and 2. the functioning of each of the main parts of the device (for example, 'Depressing the lever causes the spring to compress'). Function description is frequently associated with causality and result as the second example above shows.

7.2.3 Process description

Although process description can be characterized as a type of function description, the differences are sufficient to have it treated separately. It refers, by definition, to a series of steps or stages that are interrelated in that each step (but the first) is dependent on the preceding step and that all steps lead toward a definite goal. Often a process description is a series of instructions. However, as this type of process usually requires the imperative form of the verb, it is treated in section 7.5, 'The rhetoric of instructions'.

Whereas a function description might describe the operation of only the key elements of a device involved in a procedure and a physical description might select just those characteristics that the writer feels are important to the discussion, a process description always includes all of the steps leading toward the goal; that is, it leaves out none that might be of use to the reader.

Example 7.1 illustrates these differences in a paragraph containing all three types of description. The first and second sentences are primarily physical description, while sentences 3 and 4 mix physical and function description; however, only the 'key' parts of the device are treated but with just two of those described both physically and functionally. The remainder of the paragraph is a description of the process. While describing the procedure for using the device, the writer adds one more part, the tube cap, but leaves out entirely other, possibly equally important, parts such as those that join the various main pieces.

EXAMPLE 7.1   A PARAGRAPH COMBINING THE THREE TYPES OF DESCRIPTION

A canal bottom sampler, used in the Imperial Valley, California, canals consisted of a brass tube 2.7 centimeters in diameter and 15.2 centimeters long. At the bottom was attached a sharp steel cutting blade. The upper end of the tube was threaded into the base of a cone, the shoulder of which prevented the brass tube from sinking into the canal bed beyond the required depth. The upper end of the cone was attached to a handle of $2\frac{1}{2}$-inch pipe, made up of short sections coupled together so that the length of the handle could be varied according to the depth of the water. In taking a sample, the tube was pushed into the bottom deposit as far as the shoulder of the cone permitted. The handle was filled with water and a cap was screwed on the upper end. When the tube was withdrawn a partial vacuum was formed, which held the sample in the tube.

[Source: Submitted by a student; precise source unknown.]

Example 7.2 describes an object with almost the same function as the canal bottom sampler; however, in this example all three types of description are thoroughly mixed except for sentence 1, which contains just the name and the statement of the purpose of the object, and the final sentence, which gives us only physical description.

EXAMPLE 7.2   A PARAGRAPH OF MIXED DESCRIPTION

The Peterson Dredge was designed for use in biological work in which a sample of the fauna and bottom material of a definite area of bottom was desired. The apparatus consists of two flat-sided, straight-edged scoops hinged together and fitted with a device that holds them apart until they come in contact with the bottom. The catch is released when the line becomes slack, and the scoops close when a pull is again applied to the hoisting line. As usually constructed, the scoops measure 25 cm on their lower edges, and they are set 25 cm apart so that an area of 625 square cm is scraped by the apparatus. Since the closing of the scoops is effected by an upward pull on the sounding line, lead weights must be attached to the upper, distal portions of the scoops to insure a strong scraping action on the bottom. The total weight of the dredge is about 55 pounds.

[Source: Submitted by a student; precise source unknown.]

[Sentence 3 illustrates a problem that frequently causes confusion to even quite advanced non-native readers: the writer uses the definite article with the first mention of two nouns – 'catch' and 'line' – and he defines 'the line' only on second mention, referring to it as 'the hoisting line'. Definite article problems are discussed in some detail in chapter 8, section 8.4.]

Chart 7.1 summarizes the different kinds and amounts of information given by each type of description.

CHART 7.1   INFORMATION GIVEN BY EACH TYPE OF DESCRIPTION

1. *Physical description:* the physical characteristics of an object, and the spatial relationships of the object's parts to one another and to the whole and of the whole to other objects.

Physical characteristics include: dimension, shape, weight, color, texture, material, volume.

Spatial relationships include:

a) for general descriptions, position indicated by terms such as 'above', 'below', 'to the right', 'close to', etc.

b) for specific descriptions, position indicated by terms such as 'perpendicular to', '1 mm from the center', 'at an angle of 38°', etc.

2. *Function description:* the purpose or use of an object and the way in which each of the parts and the whole function.

   Use or purpose:

   a) of a part – 'The upper dial registers the ohms for each stage.'

   b) of the whole – 'The FBX3 calculates the incoming frequencies.'

   Function:

   a) of a part – 'Pushing lever A contracts the spring.'

   b) of the whole – 'The purpose of the device is to collect bottom flora.'

3. *Process description:* the steps of a procedure, the order in which these steps occur, and the goal of the procedure. (By definition, each step but the first is dependent on the preceding step.)

   a) Process description in paragraph form:

   'By turning on the current the teeth, or vanes, on the timer core pass by the teeth on the pole piece so that a magnetic path is established, causing a voltage pulse to be induced in the pickup coil. This voltage pulse causes TR-3 in the amplifier to conduct. This action turns TR-1 and TR-2 off, which interrupts the current flowing through the primary winding of the ignition coil. Thus, a high voltage surge is produced in the coil secondary, causing the firing of the proper spark plug.'

   [Source: Adapted from Bricker, *Automobile Guide*, p. 318.]

   b) Process description in instructions (list form):

   'The procedure for checking the operation of the current limit range is as follows:

   1. Set current limit range to 0.02A.
   2. Set the meter range switch to A.
   3. Set the decade controls to zero (000000).
   4. Connect an 8.2K, 10% 1W resistor across the output terminals.'

   [Source: *Model 382A Voltage/Current Calibrator Operator's Manual* (Seattle, Washington: Fluke Manufacturing Co., 1964), p. 4-2.]

7.3   The rhetoric of definition

There are many kinds of definitions and they come in all sizes from a single word to entire books. The kinds of definitions we are usually concerned with in written EST discourse are fortunately among the shortest and simplest. They also appear in our discourse very frequently, especially in elementary texts such as training manuals, textbooks for beginners in a field, etc. We find them also in more advanced discourse; in fact, when writers present new concepts, or when new technology needs explanation, or when someone is describing a new way of looking at an old idea. All of these require definitions ranging from a word to, at times, several paragraphs.

Our research into EST discourse yielded two broad categories of definition – simple definition and complex (or expanded) definition. Simple definition, by which we mean a definition completed in one sentence or less, we divide into three basic types: formal definition, semi-formal definition, and non-formal definition. Each of these provides information in different amounts and at different levels of precision. The formal definition gives us the most and the most precise information; the semi-formal definition, while it leaves out one important item, gives us almost as much information with almost as much precision; and the non-formal definition gives us considerably less information and a good deal less precision.

The rhetorical process was originally designed to deal only with simple definition, since it was the most common category in EST discourse. However, when we realized the frequency of occurrence of more complex forms of definition, we found that we could work with these as well by applying some of the procedures used in the analysis of paragraphs and rhetorical techniques. These more complex forms of definition we usually call 'expanded' definition and, in certain cases, 'special types' of definition. Characteristically, most expanded definitions are developed in paragraph units and have, as a rule, a simple definition – formal or semi-formal – for their core statement. The most common types of expansion are those incorporating other rhetorical functions (for example, description or classification) along with some of the rhetorical techniques such as time or space order, causality and result, contrast, etc. The special types we treat in this book are definition by stipulation, definition by explication, and definition by operation.

7.3.1   Formal definition

Theoretically, a formal definition gives the most information and the most precise information of any of the three types of simple definition. It is, of course, the well-known equation-like *'Species = Genus +*

Differentia', usually called 'formal' because of its rigidity of form. We have kept the term but expanded its definition by adding the amount and kind of information it includes. When teaching formal definition we avoid the Latin terms and use English ones, starting with an equation $T = C + D$, and defining it as follows: T is the *term* being defined; C is the *class* (or 'set') of which the term is a member ('subset'); and D is the sum of the *differences* given to distinguish this term from all other members of the class. This is a great deal of information to get from a single sentence and the learner, especially the non-native learner, often needs to have pointed out just how much information can be drawn from this small bit of discourse.

An example we find very useful is the formal definition of 'arachnid': 'An arachnid is an invertebrate animal having (or, which has) eight legs extending at equal intervals from a central body.' The three pieces of information in this definition are:

1. T, the term, = *arachnid*
2. C, the class, = *invertebrate animal*
3. D, the differences (that is, the differences between our term and all other invertebrate animals) =
   a) an arachnid has eight legs, and
   b) these extend at equal intervals from a central body.

Both of these differences are necessary since other invertebrate animals – the octopods – also have eight legs; however, the arachnid is (insofar as we know) the only eight-legged invertebrate animal that has its legs extending at equal intervals from a central body.

Because of the importance of the relationship of the items of information in a formal definition to one another as well as to the process of classification, it is useful to point out these relationships to students: first, we have the term, a name (and one which may be new in the reader's experience); second, we have the name of a group (class or set) into which the term fits, thus possibly giving us another new word and certainly a new set of relationships (between the term and the class); and third, we have some vital characteristics that definitely identify our term and at the same time separate it from its siblings – the other members of its class. Although it is possible to have a virtually unlimited string of differences in a one-sentence formal definition, writers seldom go beyond the limits of acceptable sentence structure. Instead, when they need (or want) to add to the precision of their definitions by giving additional information, writers usually expand their material to a paragraph – with as many physical paragraphs as are necessary – and with the original defining sentence as the core statement. Expansion of definitions is discussed below in sub-section 7.3.4, 'Complex definition'.

A fruitful approach with students studying science or technology is to show the relationship of the items of information through diagrams whenever possible. In working with definition and, as we will see later, with classification, diagrams are a very useful adjunct to a standard class discussion. Chart 7.2 is the type of definition diagram we find applicable to students on all levels of subject-matter knowledge, from beginning to advanced, and on levels of English ability from lower intermediate on.

CHART 7.2   FORMAL DEFINITION DIAGRAMS

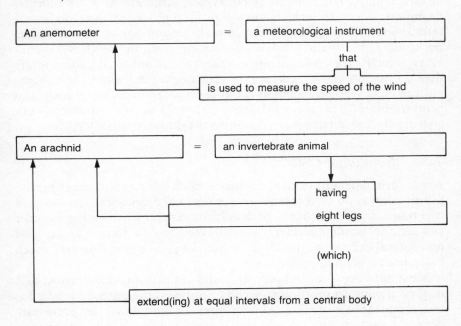

7.3.2 Semi-formal definition

Although semi-formal definitions presumably provide the reader with less information than do formal definitions, this is not always true. By definition, a semi-formal definition contains only two of the three basic defining elements: the term being defined and the statement of differences. 'Semi-formal' refers to the form of the definition, and indicates that it is not complete: the class is left out.

As a rule, writers will leave out a statement of class not because they are forgetful, careless, or bad writers but because the class is assumed to be either obvious (that is, the idea of the class is contained in the term being defined) or is so large as to be meaningless. For example, in the first instance, if the term being defined ends in '-logy', there is little point in telling the reader that it is a member of a class called 'science'; in the second, a class such as 'device' or 'science' is too large to carry much genuine information to a reader. In cases such as these, a semi-formal definition really brings readers as much information as a fully formal definition.

However, there are many occasions when semi-formal definitions do not provide as much information as a formal definition nor, for that matter, even all of the information necessary to give the reader adequate 'defining information'. If we drop the class from our previous definition of 'arachnid', what remains is the typical structure of a semi-formal definition: 'An arachnid has eight legs projecting at equal intervals from a central body.' This is clearly a definition by description of all arachnidae, but it leaves out the important information given by the class 'invertebrate animal'. We could, as some writers of definitions do, incorporate the information in the class into the statement of differences: 'An arachnid has eight legs extending at equal intervals from a central body and is invertebrate.' This way of defining obviously has its limitations, both stylistically and in terms of overloading the statement of differences.

7.3.3   Non-formal definition

A non-formal definition gives neither as much information nor as precise information as do either formal or semi-formal definitions. The function of a non-formal definition is to define in a general sense so that a reader can see the familiar element in whatever the new term may be. The non-formal definition, therefore, is not designed to provide very much basic, precise defining information.

Most non-formal definitions are found in the form of synonyms; that is, they attempt to substitute a word or phrase familiar to the reader for one presumably unfamiliar. A non-formal definition of our previously defined term 'arachnid' would be 'An arachnid is a spider.' In terms of precision of statement, this definition is not, strictly speaking, true. A spider is merely one kind of arachnid; thus, the definition is not substituting a term that is on the same level of generality as the term being defined. This is a weakness of many definitions by synonym. However, since precision is not the writer's interest here and since a spider is the most well known form of arachnid, the definition quite adequately satisfies its purpose of giving readers enough of an idea of the meaning of 'arachnid' that they can continue reading with little, if any, loss of comprehension.

From the above we can see that one type of non-formal definition gives a term in the form of a class and then defines by naming a common member of the class. On a more formal level this would be 'A spider is an arachnid which. . . .' A second frequently found method of defining non-formally is to give a term and then define it by its most common (or most outstanding) characteristic. We can define 'helix' in this way as 'A helix is a spiral.' Although any spiral form or structure can be called a helix, not all helixes are spiral; some are cylindrical, for example. Our definition of 'helix', then, gives a characteristic of the most common form of helix rather than a true synonym.

Non-formal definition has its place even in EST discourse, where precision of statement is of major importance. Learners, however, need to be taught to recognize the difference in the amounts and preciseness of information given by each type of definition. They should not, for instance, assume that a statement such as 'An arachnid (spider)....' provides as much precise information as one of the more formal forms of definition of the same term.

The other forms of non-formal definition are 1. definition by negative statement and 2. definition by antonym. We can define arachnid negatively with the statement 'An arachnid is not an insect', although to many this is not a definition at all. We also find a kind of negative in definition by antonym: 'The opposite of indigenous is foreign.' While this can be a useful means of defining, especially when there is no well-known 'positive' word to use as a synonym, it is unfortunately too often misused by writers who fail to follow the basic logic of the relationship between a term being defined and its definition. A definition must be more well known (or simpler) than the term being defined. The problem is obvious when we get definitions such as 'The opposite of foreign is indigenous', or by synonym, 'Native means indigenous.' This is the type of definition too often found in those small bilingual dictionaries non-native students tend to carry in their pockets. We find it worthwhile to warn students against dictionaries of this type, especially when they (commonly) put in such definitions as 'tautological' means 'redundant' and then go on to define 'redundant' as 'tautological'. Chart 7.3 is a summary of the kinds and amounts of information given by each type of definition.

CHART 7.3   INFORMATION GIVEN BY TYPES OF DEFINITIONS

   I.   *Formal definition.* A formal definition gives the reader three kinds of information:
        1. The name of the *term* being defined.
        2. The *class* to which the term belongs (i.e., the set of which the term is a subset).
        3. The *difference(s)* between the term and all other members of the class: these differences are essential characteristics of the term (essential in respect to the subject under discussion).

   II. *Semi-formal definition.* A semi-formal definition gives the reader two kinds of information:
        1. The name of the *term* being defined.
        2. The *difference(s)* between the term and the other members of the class. (This class is not stated; it is often assumed by

the writer either to be obvious or to be of no importance to the discussion.)

III. *Non-formal definition.* A non-formal definition gives the reader two kinds of information:
   1. The name of the *term* being defined.
   2. Another word or phrase having the approximate meaning of the term, or giving an outstanding characteristic of the term. (This word or phrase can be stated positively, as a synonym, or negatively, as an antonym; in either case, it does not carry defining information as precise as that of the other two types of simple definition.)

Each of the types of definition discussed above is illustrated in example 7.3.

EXAMPLE 7.3   EXAMPLES OF THE THREE TYPES OF SIMPLE DEFINITION

I. Formal definition
   1. developed by physical description:
      'An arachnid is an invertebrate animal having eight legs extending at equal intervals from a central body.'
   2. developed by function description:
      'An anemometer is a meteorological instrument that registers the speed of the wind on a dial or gage.'
   3. developed by use/purpose:
      'An anemometer is a meteorological instrument that is used to measure the speed of the wind.'

II. Semi-formal definition
   1. containing physical descriptive information:
      'An arachnid has eight legs extending at equal intervals from a central body.'
   2. containing descriptive information:
      'An anemometer registers the speed of the wind on a dial or gage.'
   3. containing information on use/purpose:
      'An anemometer is used to measure the speed of the wind.'

III. Non-formal definition
   1. by synonym:
      'An arachnid is a spider.'/'An arachnid (spider)....'
   2. by antonym:
      'The opposite of indigenous is foreign.'
      [NOT 'The opposite of foreign is indigenous.']

7.3.4   *Complex definition*

This category of definition includes those special types that are found most often in written EST discourse. These are definition 1. by stipulation, 2. by operation, and 3. by explication. We occasionally find definition by stipulation in a single sentence; however, as a rule all three are forms of expanded definition and so are found in full paragraphs or even in groups of paragraphs. In addition, we frequently find that EST texts use several other ways of expanding definitions. These are discussed below along with the three special types of definition.

Stipulation. Stipulatory definitions are found only in connection with other types of definition which are usually (but not necessarily) formal in form. The purpose of a stipulating definition is to set limits – in time, in place, in field, in meaning – to the main definition. For example, in our discussion of paragraph we stipulated (note 4, chapter 3) that 'paragraph' meant 'conceptual paragraph'; that is, we limited the meaning of the term being defined.

In written EST discourse, we find three types of stipulatory definition: mathematical stipulation, legal stipulation, and 'general' stipulation, this last so called because we find it commonly throughout English discourse, not just in EST. Each type of stipulation is illustrated in example 7.4.

EXAMPLE 7.4   SPECIAL TYPES OF DEFINITION: STIPULATION

1. *Mathematical stipulation* is used mostly to identify the symbols in a formula or an equation or to set values to variables:
   'In this formula X represents the vertical vector.'
   'Pi, in this equation, has the value of 3.14159.'

2. *Legal stipulation* is found mostly in contracts and similar business documents:
   'The term "special tooling", *as used in this clause*, includes all jigs, dies, fixtures, molds, patterns ... and other special articles of equipment.'

[Source: Quoted in H. M. Weisman, *Basic Technical Writing* (Columbus, Ohio: Merrill, 1962), p. 135.]

3. *General stipulation* is used frequently in EST discourse when scientists coin names for discoveries; or assign new terms, or apply old terms in new ways, to activities, processes or objects resulting from research and similar investigations:
   'In information theory, "entropy" means "information" or "freedom of information source".'

Operation. An operational definition tells the reader what to do in order to experience – physically and/or mentally – whatever is being defined. Most (though not all) operational definitions in written EST discourse refer to a physical, usually mechanical, activity. Often the text of the definition will contain a set of instructions, but with the verbs usually in the indicative rather than in the imperative. Example 7.5 illustrates two different styles of operational definition. Note that in each the discourse begins with a definition: the first is a formal definition of the 'sound [f]'; the second contains all the formal elements but is not stated in formal definition terms. In the case of the first example, we have a single sentence definition with the 'operational' element coming in the statement of differences. This type of operational definition – with the entire definition in a single sentence – is not at all common since most texts of this type would go on and develop the information in at least one paragraph. The second example has a definition as the core statement of its paragraph and the supporting details in the form of operational information.

EXAMPLE 7.5   SPECIAL TYPES OF DEFINITION: OPERATION

1. *An operational definition in one sentence:* 'The sound [f] is a voiceless, labio-dental fricative, formed by placing the lower lip lightly against the upper teeth, closing the vellum, and forcing the breath out through the spaces between the teeth or between the teeth and the upper lip.'

[Source: Quoted in H. M. Weisman, *Basic Technical Writing*, p. 136.]

2. *A more typical operational definition* (one requiring at least a paragraph for full development): 'Torque, in a motor, is a measure of how much load the motor can turn or lift. On small motors, torque is measured in inch-ounces. A simple way to determine torque is to wrap a cord around a pulley secured to the shaft, then add small weights until the motor is no longer capable of lifting the load.'

[Source: Quoted in H. M. Weisman, *Basic Technical Writing*, p. 136.]

[Note: The operational part of the definition begins with sentence 3. The definition (also the core statement) is formal in that it provides three kinds of information: the term is 'torque'; the class, 'measure'; the difference, 'how much load. . . .' The stipulation 'in a motor' limits this particular definition of torque to a motor; that is, the definition does not necessarily apply to other mechanical devices.]

Explication. Definition by explication is found as a rule in elementary-level EST discourse (beginning textbooks, manuals for apprentices, etc.). The purpose of an explicated definition is to give the reader new information about the key terms in the original definition. This new information is usually in the form of synonyms – words and/or phrases – that substitute for the original defining words or phrases that the writer wishes to clarify. An excellent illustration of a writer clarifying an original definition for the benefit of readers presumably new to the subject area being defined is example 4.4 along with the adapted version in example 4.5A. Dr Nourse uses additional physical paragraphs to explicate the key terms in his statement of differences and, to give the reader even more information, he also explicates the class, 'process'. Our illustration of an explicated definition (example 7.6) is much simpler, consisting of a formal definition followed by two sentences, each explicating one of the key phrases in the statement of differences.

EXAMPLE 7.6   SPECIAL TYPES OF DEFINITION: EXPLICATION

> The two key phrases explicated in this definition are 'soil management' and 'crop production':
> 'Agronomy is a science which seeks improved methods of soil management and crop production. By crop production we mean new techniques that will increase the yield of field crops. By improved soil management we mean the use of fertilizers which contain the necessary nutrients needed for the crops.'

[Source: Submitted by a student; precise source unknown.]

Other ways of expanding definitions. In addition to the expansion of the special types of definitions, writers often add information to other types of simple definition by expanding these into paragraphs, again with the initial definitions usually the core statements of those paragraphs. As a rule the writers use the rhetorical functions of description and classification and the rhetorical technique of exemplification as their main methods of expansion. Each of these three methods is illustrated in example 7.7.

EXAMPLE 7.7   OTHER WAYS OF EXPANDING DEFINITIONS

> 1. *Expansion by description*
>   'A source is a device that selects and transmits sequences of symbols from a given alphabet. Each selection is made at random. The channel transmits the incoming signal to the receiver....'

[Source: F. M. Reza, *An Introduction to Information Theory* (New York: McGraw-Hill, 1960), p. 3.]

[The expansion of the formal definition is by function description (statement of differences and sentence 2) and then by process description (the remaining sentences of the paragraph, of which only the first is given here). The writer uses the formal definition as his core statement. He could not leave out the class ('device') as would normally be the case since the word 'source' is not usually thought of as something mechanical. To write 'A source selects and transmits . . .' would not have given the reader adequate information.]

2. *Expansion by classification*
   'The triode is a standard vacuum tube [which is] used where signal to noise ratio is not critical. Other standard vacuum tubes are the tetrode, the pentode, and the multi-unit. The tetrode is used where medium signal amplification is desired. The pentode is used . . ./The multi-unit is used. . . .' (See example 7.10 for full text.)

[The class in this definition is 'standard vacuum tube' and it is this class that is expanded by listing its other important members (important, that is, to the writer's subject). The information on each of the members of the class is in terms of use; this choice is governed by the statement of difference also being in terms of use. The detailed discussion of classification is in section 7.4.]

3. *Expansion by exemplification*
   'The average physical product is a measure of efficiency which is determined by the total output divided by the total number of variable inputs used to produce that level of output. For example, if two variable inputs are required to produce four units of output, the average physical product (and hence the measure of efficiency at that level of production) is two units of output per unit of variable input.'

[Source: Written by a student.]

[The expansion of the definition is not, as in the previous examples an expansion of the statement of differences or of the class but of the term itself. As this paragraph is designed, the expansion takes the generalized statement of differences and makes it specific, thus illustrating directly the term being defined.]

7.4   The rhetoric of classification

To this point we have seen classification used in the development of both describing and defining paragraphs. In addition to this supplementary role, classification is frequently the main function of paragraphs and so is capable of being isolated and studied on its own.

In our work with written EST discourse we found that classification is actually a two-way process: if we have one or more members of a class, the procedure is to find the class (and give it a name) to which those members belong; if we have a class (named), we then try to find the members that make up this class. This latter procedure is more properly called 'analysis'; however, for purposes of identifying the process of classification in reading EST discourse and in using it in writing, we find it better to teach the two procedures as simply two parts of the same process. (Note that taking a device or an object and breaking it into its component parts is neither classification nor analysis. It is a part of the process of physical description and is correctly called 'partition'.)

Most EST discourse classifies in the true sense of the term: it begins with one or more apparently related items and looks for the larger group that these might fit into. However, at times we get both procedures operating together: after finding a class for an item (or items) we then find it necessary to determine what other items, if any, are also members of this class. Further, as we shall see, we find classification existing simultaneously at more than one level: a term which is a class at one level may well be a member of a class at a higher level and the member of a class at one level may well be the class of the level one step down, with level, of course, meaning 'level of generality'. The expression of these relationships – putting order into our universe – is one of the most common functions of EST discourse.

Classification is worth spending teaching time on since, like definition, it is so basic to human thinking and to scientific expression. Also, classification is concerned with levels of generalization and of related specifics. It is always surprising to discover how few students – whether native or non-native – realize that a generalization at one level of a classification can be a specific at another; nor do they always realize the relationship between classes and members of those classes at different levels. This problem is discussed in detail in sub-section 7.4.3; here it is enough to point out that to have students orally make several levels of classification about familiar things easy to classify – cars, sports, stereo systems, etc. – is not only a useful exercise, it is one that invariably generates a good deal of student interest.

Another approach to teaching classification is through definition. These are such closely related functions that when a formal definition is written on the blackboard (or on a handout) and a statement of classification (using the same terms) is written directly beneath it, we find that most students very quickly see the relationships between the two and equally quickly are able to verbalize them.

We find two essential differences between the rhetorical functions of formal definition and classification: the first is that definition deals with only one member of a class while classification deals with all (or the most important) members; the second is that the statement of difference in a formal definition has as its purpose the isolation of the term being defined, while its counterpart in classification, usually called the 'basis for (or criterion of) classification', has the purpose of naming something that is shared by all members of the class. The meaning of the term 'basis for classification' is discussed in detail in sub-section 7.4.1.

In our work with EST discourse we identified three types of classification: 1. complete classification, 2. partial classification, and 3. implicit classification. Each of the three types, as with the basic types of simple definition, provides us with different amounts of information. Implicit classification, however, like implicit definition, is determined by the way in which the classifying information is expressed by the discourse; that is, it is implicit if it is classifying information stated other than in classification terms. (See chart 7.4 for a summary of information given by types of classification.)

7.4.1   Complete classification

To be complete, a classification must provide the reader with three kinds of information, although not necessarily in this order:
1. the item (or items) being classified – i.e., the members of the class
2. the class to which the items (members) belong
3. the basis (or bases) for classification

The first gives us the names of two or more terms and suggests that there is a relationship between them but does not specify precisely what this relationship is. (Note that if a class only has one member, then the member and the class are the same and we do not have a true classification.) The second names the class to which the members belong and gives us additional information on the relationship between them. The third tells us in what way (or ways) the members of the class differ from one another and may also tell us in what way (or ways) they are similar – that is, how they are related – although this information may be suggested by the class itself.

We find all three kinds of information in the following one sentence classification: 'We can classify particles into three types in respect to size: 1. those easily visible to the naked eye; 2. those which cannot be distinguished even under powerful optical microscopes; and 3. those molecules of a substance like water or sugar.' First, we are told that we are to be given a classification; then our classifying information comes in the following order: the class (particles), how many members the class will have, on what basis these differ from one another (size), and then more specific descriptions of this difference.

In this example we have what is called a 'closed class'; that is, a class which has only those members listed. Other types of classes worth discussing are the open-ended (infinite) class and the closed class that has a finite number of members, only some of which are essential to any given discussion. Many closed classes have more members than are ever named by writers making a classification: in such cases, the writers choose only those members that are pertinent to the subject under discussion. For example, we might have a class called 'fasteners'. It has a finite number of members since there are only so many kinds of 'fasteners'. Some of these members are 'nails', 'wood screws', 'metal screws', 'nuts and bolts', 'staples', 'paper clips', and 'brads'. Unless someone writing about 'fasteners' was attempting to do a complete survey, a classification would list only those members that dealt with the fastening of particular materials: for example, wood or paper or metal sheeting.

There are innumerable examples of open-ended classes – those with an infinite number of members (or at least more members than we are capable of counting): any type of constantly changing population, such as bacteria, viruses, or the number of people in any given country; the stars in the universe, etc. Obviously, it would be impossible for writers to list all the members of such classes, even if they wanted to do so. Examples 7.8A, B, and C illustrate both open-ended and closed complete classifications.

EXAMPLE 7.8A   A COMPLETE CLASSIFICATION WITH A FINITE
NUMBER OF MEMBERS

> All crystalline solids can be classified as members of one of
> fourteen crystal systems. The number of ways in which atomic
> arrangements can be repeated to form a solid is limited to fourteen
> by the geometries of space division. Any one of these
> arrangements, when repeated in space, forms the lattice structure
> characteristic of a crystalline material. These fourteen systems
> are. . . . For example, cadmium sulphide has a lattice formed of
> hexagonal units. . . .

> [Source: Adapted from Sir Nevill Mott, 'The Solid State', *Scientific American*,
> September 1967, p. 83.]

> [This example has two levels of classification: the largest class is
> 'crystalline systems', which has 'fourteen crystal systems' as its
> members. These crystal systems become classes in turn, each of which
> has an unspecified number of crystalline solids for its members. The

second sentence gives us the basis for classification of the fourteen members of the class 'crystalline systems'. The next to last sentence names the fourteen members of this class, and the final sentence gives us an example (one member) of one of the second level classes; that is, a member of one of the fourteen systems that have become classes after first having been members of a larger class. We are also given the name of this member: 'hexagonal units'.]

EXAMPLE 7.8B   A COMPLETE CLASSIFICATION WITH MORE
THAN ONE STATED BASIS

We can classify the planets of our solar system by one or more of the following characteristics: average distance from sun, Earth = 1; solar radiation received, Earth = 1; orbital period; eccentricity; equatorial diameter in miles; mass, Earth = 1; gravity, Earth = 1; escape velocity in mi/sec.; rotation period; inclination in degrees; and albedo.

[Source: Adapted from George Ohring, *Weather on the Planets*, Science Study Series, S47 (New York: Doubleday, 1966), pp. 30–1.]

[Although the writer does not name the planets at this point, he does so elsewhere in the book. He follows this paragraph by defining several of the characteristics he lists. While he does not tell the reader that the characteristic chosen determines the order in which the members should be listed, it is a point worth mentioning during discussion of the rhetoric of classification. For example, if the criterion (basis) chosen is 'average distance from the sun', Earth would be third, assuming that the first named is the closest planet to the sun. On the other hand, if the basis is 'equatorial diameter in miles', Earth would be fifth, as there are four planets (if we include Pluto) with smaller equatorial diameters.]

EXAMPLE 7.8C   AN OPEN-ENDED CLASSIFICATION

In the many types of service conditions in which refractories are used, there is a great variety of different kinds of abrasion. The destructive action of abrasion on a furnace lining may be the result of scraping, scouring, gouging, rubbing, impingement of relatively fine particles of material, or impact of heavy objects. For convenience in discussing the various types of abrasive action, we can classify abrasion under three general headings, namely:
1. Abrasion by rubbing
2. Abrasion by impingement
3. Abrasion by impact

[Source: Report on 'Abrasion' quoted in Gordon H. Mills and John A. Walter, *Technical Writing*, 3rd edn (New York: Holt, Rinehart and Winston, 1970), n.p.]

[The basis for classification is not given in so many words; however, it is clear from the writer's statements that the basis is 'the differing actions of the "different kinds of abrasion"'. While it is probable that 'abrasion' is a finite class with a countable number of members, the writer here treats it as open-ended and lists those he considers the most important types of abrasion. Since he lists three others, we have an unstated second level of classification with these subsumed under one of the 'general' types of abrasion.]

7.4.2   Partial classification

Whether the class is open or closed, it is considered complete only if the basis is stated (as in examples 7.8A and B) or is clear from the context (as in example 7.8C). Classification that leaves out the basis for classifying is called partial classification. Writers usually fail to state the basis because they feel that it is obvious (or, unfortunately, because they are sometimes poor writers). Example 7.9 illustrates a paragraph of classification that has no stated basis because the writer felt that this was obvious from the context.

EXAMPLE 7.9   A PARTIAL CLASSIFICATION WITH ITS BASIS
UNSTATED BUT OBVIOUS

A triode is a standard vacuum tube which contains three electrodes: an anode, a cathode, and a control electrode called the grid. Other standard vacuum tubes are: tetrode, pentode, and multi-unit. The tetrode is a four electrode electron tube containing the three elements which the triode has plus one additional element: This is ordinarily a screen grid. The tetrode is used where medium signal amplification is desired. With the addition of a fifth element, the resulting tube is called a pentode. The pentode is used in circuitry where high amplification is desired. The multi-unit tube has two or more separate tubes in one shell. It is used as a space saver because it contains two tubes in one.

[Source: Written by a non-native advanced undergraduate engineering student for an in-class exercise in classification, University of Washington (Seattle), HSS 304, Winter Quarter, 1978.]

[Since the writer does not explicitly give the basis for classification, this is called a partial classification. Actually all three of the requirements for a complete classification are obvious from the context, especially since the classification starts with a formal definition of one member, thus establishing the name of a member, the class, and how this member differs from the others (as yet unnamed) in the class. Using this information, the writer carries the reader quickly into the classification of vacuum tubes by naming three other important members of the class. Thus by the end of the second sentence, we have all of the basic information needed: the class, the members of the class, and – from the formal definition – a clear statement of difference, which later suggests (but does not state) the basis for classification; that is, the number of electrodes differs for each member of the class. A one-sentence example of a partial classification that is helpful to use in the beginning of the discussion is 'Razor blades can be classified as single edge or double edge.' Here we have the name of the class and of its two members but no statement of the basis for classification, although this is quite obvious. Even so, we find it worthwhile to ask the students to make the classification complete by providing a basis for classification. A typical answer would be, 'Razor blades can be classified according to the number of edges a blade has. There are single-edged and double-edged blades.']

7.4.3 Implicit classification

Implicit classification refers to classifying information that is present in the discourse but not in classification terms. Above, we noted that the basis for classification in a partial classification is often present in the text but not stated explicitly as the basis. In an implicit classification all of the classifying information is present but is not stated as such. Nor does the paragraph have classification as its rhetorical function. Just as with implicit definition readers can be taught to find the classifying information in a paragraph that does not have the overt purpose of classifying and they can also be taught to abstract out this information and rearrange it in classificatory form.

Example 7.10A is fairly typical of implicit classifications found in elementary science and technology textbooks. There are a number of ways that students can be helped to learn how to abstract out the necessary classifying information from a piece of discourse of this type. One way is to write down the names of each of the items of information expected from a classification, follow each name with a blank and then find terms and phrases that fit the names and so fill in the blanks. This is both a sound in-class exercise and one for learners to do with their own subject-matter reading.

EXAMPLE 7.10A   A PARAGRAPH CONTAINING SIMPLE IMPLICIT CLASSIFICATION

The Three States of Matter

In the solid state a body has definite volume and is almost incompressible. It also has a shape independent of the space in which it is placed. As considerable force is necessary to separate portions of it, it is said to possess considerable cohesion. In the liquid state matter also possesses a definite volume and has little compressibility, but it has no definite shape and automatically takes the shape of any vessel into which it is placed. Also a liquid shows much less cohesion than a solid. In the gaseous state matter has neither fixed volume nor fixed shape. A quantity of gas introduced into any closed space immediately spreads out to fill that space. Also a gas shows considerable compressibility and has practically no cohesion.

[Source: Submitted by a student; precise source unknown.]

[Using the information in the above example, we can fill in the classification chart described above as follows:

CLASS: _____States of matter_____

MEMBERS OF THE CLASS: ____Solids, liquids, gases_____

BASIS (BASES) FOR
CLASSIFICATION: ____Compressibility, definiteness_____
_____of shape, volume, cohesion_____

A more visual and often more functional way for readers to record the classifying information from an implicit classification is to put the information in the form of 'trees', as shown in the two paragraphs of example 7.10B. This 'tree' method of recording the results of analysis of texts for classifying information we find to be most useful for the students, both in the classroom and outside, when they need to analyze their subject-matter reading. A 'classification tree' follows immediately after each paragraph.]

EXAMPLE 7.10B   TWO PARAGRAPHS ILLUSTRATING IMPLICIT CLASSIFICATION

Paragraph 1: Simple implicit classification
Underground water reserves are much larger than those on the surface, but as they are unseen we tend to underestimate them. It is vitally important that we make use of these underground reserves, but never haphazardly. For example, where does the water come from which we find in one or another of the underground water-bearing layers (aquifers)? How does it move? How is it renewed? And, if this water is used, what effect will it have on the discharge and future level of the water table? What are the laws of hydrology? Despite the immense progress of recent years, all of these questions still have not been fully answered.

[Source: M. Batisse, *Courier* (UNESCO, July–August 1964); quoted in J. R. Ewer and G. Latorre, *A Course in Basic Scientific English* (London: Longman, 1969), p. 123.]

The rhetorical functions

Classification tree:

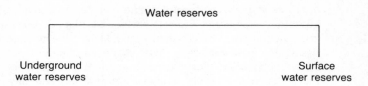

[Basis for classification: location of water reserves]

Paragraph 2: Complex implicit classification

A similar need for research exists in the branch of hydrology that deals with the quality of water. In nature, there is no water like the pure water defined by chemists, made up of only hydrogen and oxygen. River water, ground water, and even rain water always contain other dissolved or suspended elements, and these, even when present in small quantities, play an important role.

[Source: Batisse, in Ewer and Latorre, pp. 123–4.]

Classification tree:

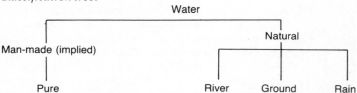

[For the bases for classification of the three classes in the above complex classification tree, see the discussion in the following paragraph.

This example of complex implicit classification has two levels of generality: the class of the first (highest) level is 'water', with the two members 'man-made' and 'natural', 'man-made water' being implied by the second sentence of the paragraph. Dropping down to the second level, we find that the members of the first level have become classes on the second level. The class 'man-made' is shown with only one member; however, since chemists can obviously make other kinds of water along with 'pure water', we can also imply additional members: 'impure water', 'saline water', 'heavy water', etc. Also, the writer gives us only three members of the class 'natural (water)' even though there are several other natural sources. Finally, although he fails to give us the bases for classification for any of the three classes, we can easily supply these from context: at the first level, we clearly have as the basis for classification, 'How the various kinds of water are produced'; and at the second level we have 'quality of water' as the basis for the class 'man-made', and 'sources' as the basis for 'natural'.[1]]

The kinds and amounts of information given by the three types of classification discussed above are summarized in chart 7.4.

CHART 7.4   INFORMATION GIVEN BY TYPES OF
CLASSIFICATION

I.   *Complete classification.* A complete classification gives the reader three kinds of information:
   1. The name of the class (that is, the set)
   2. The members of the class (that is, the sub-sets of the set) – sometimes writers give all members of the class; at other times they give only those members pertinent to the subject. This is especially true when the subject of the discourse is such that the class has a very large number of members or is non-finite.
   3. The basis (or bases) for classification – that is, the characteristics of each member that are similar and those that are different. Sometimes only the differences are stated: the similarities are then implied in the class.

II.   *Partial classification.* A partial classification gives the reader two kinds of information:
   1. The name of the class
   2. The members of the class (as above)

[A partial classification leaves out the basis for classification either because the writer assumes that the information will be obvious to the reader or is not important to the discussion.]

III.   *Implicit classification.* An implicit classification is found in a piece of discourse that has a rhetorical function other than classification. Most implicit classifications contain all three kinds of information listed under 'Complete classification' above, although it is not stated in classifying terms. Context usually provides the information in such a way that it can be easily abstracted from the text and put into a classification chart or in the form of a classification tree so that the reader can more easily see the whole and, therefore, the relationships of the information in the classification to other information in the discourse.

7.4.4   *Classification as a process*

On the surface, classification seems a simple enough concept to be taught in the classroom with little difficulty. Having the students find examples in their reading poses few if any problems: virtually all scientific and technical discourse contains samples of classification. However, we discovered early in our work that even though the students bring excellent examples to class, they are not always able to interpret these as easily and fully as they can their examples of definition and description. Many students recognize that they are dealing with more than one level of generality but are unable to discuss these in a way that shows they have gained the necessary insights into the concepts involved. This is, as to be expected, especially true when they are dealing with implicit classification.

We devised the following solution: first, we get the students to recognize explicit classifications that have only one level. Once we feel satisfied that they have grasped the basic principles involved we get them to produce their own paragraphs of explicit classification. This approach is not simply a matter of telling the students to use as models the paragraphs handed out as examples or those from their own subject-matter reading. To classify well requires more understanding of the concept of classification than does just recognizing that a writer is classifying. For this reason, we give the students a set of 'rules' to use when writing paragraphs of classification. These rules are fairly obvious; yet it is surprising how often they are not followed even by 'published' writers. If they are not followed (or are followed 'badly'), the result can be an unordered mishmash of details or, at the very best, an example of fuzzy thinking. This set of 'rules' is summarized in chart 7.5 and discussed in more detail in chapter 10.

CHART 7.5   SUMMARY OF RULES FOR CLASSIFYING

1. Writers must be able to define their class and each member of that class. They should understand the relation of the class and the members to one another and to the 'outside world'.
2. A class must have at least two members. If a class has only one member, then that member and the class are the same. In implicit classification some or all members may have to be reconstructed from 'logic' as well as context.
3. In large classes it is not usually necessary nor advisable to state all members. With these and with 'infinite' classes, writers must decide which members to list for the readers.
4. All members of a class must have at least one characteristic in common: this commonality is the basis for their all being members of the same class.
5. Each member of a class must be clearly separated from all other members by the basis (bases) for classification which functions to differentiate them from each other.
6. Classification must be made on only one level at a time. Mixing levels is a sure sign of lack of understanding of the principles of classification.

Many students tend to confuse the process of 'partition' with that of classification. Partition is the process of breaking an object into its component parts and naming each part – or, at the very least, naming each important part. Partition, then, is related to the rhetorical function of physical description and the rhetorical technique of space order. The difference between partition and classification in respect to teaching is given in some detail in chapter 10.

7.5   The rhetoric of instructions

Although we find the rhetoric of instructions exemplified in both academic and occupational English discourse (see charts 2.1 and 2.2, p. 6), by their very nature instructions are found more in occupational English. In academic discourse instructions are confined primarily to assignments in textbooks, to laboratory manuals for science and engineering students, and to occasional uses in peer writing.

While there is often a marked difference between instructions for technicians and for academic personnel, there is also a broad area of overlap. This overlap is most easily seen in those laboratory and other manuals used by both trained technicians in research facilities and by academics – students and teachers – in laboratories. It is illustrated by example 7.11, which is from a manual used by highly trained technicians and by electrical engineering professors and their advanced undergraduate and graduate students.

EXAMPLE 7.11   INSTRUCTIONS USED BY BOTH OCCUPATIONAL
AND ACADEMIC PERSONNEL

> Operation of the VOLTAGE LIMIT control can be checked as follows:
> 1. Set the VOLTAGE LIMIT control to mid-range.
> 2. Set the V-A switch to 5 ma.
> 3. Connect a 10K, 5%, $\frac{1}{2}$W resistor across the OUTPUT terminals.
> 4. Connect the 881A to the OUTPUT terminals.
> 5. Set the decade controls to 4.000000 ma.
> 6. Set POWER switch to ON.
> 7. Set the VOLTAGE LIMIT to a minimum. The 881A should indicate that the output voltage decreases to below 5 volts.

[Source: *Model 382A Voltage/Current Calibrator Operator's Manual* (Seattle, Washington: Fluke Manufacturing Co., 1964), p. 4-3.]

[This text assumes that the user already knows the various controls and can read the 'code' terms, such as 88A, V-A switch, OUTPUT terminals, decade controls, and power switch. In manuals that are for learners (apprentices, hobbyists, etc.) most of the terminology would be defined or identified by a labelled illustration.]

7.5.1 Nature of the discourse of instructions

The rhetoric of instructions provides readers with two quite different kinds of information: the first we call simply instructions; the second, instructional information. Instructions are of two types: direct instructions, which are characterized by the use of the imperative form of the verbs, and indirect instructions, which are characterized by the use of modal verbs, the passive mood, and – most frequently – a combination of the two; that is, passive modals. These are treated in detail in chapter 8.

We define instructions as discourse that tells someone to do (or not to do) something. In direct instructions, this discourse is usually in the form of a vertical list that is most often headed by a statement indicating the goal of the instructions. In indirect instructions (unless mixed in with a list of direct instructions) the discourse is usually in paragraph form, often with the core statement of the paragraph indicating the goal of the instructions. Instructional information is discourse that 'assists' instructions by providing corollary information: cautions, warnings, specifying statements, descriptions, and theoretical considerations. Example 7.12 illustrates the two kinds of instructions and instructional information in the same text. Chart 7.6 following summarizes the kinds and amounts of information given by each type of instruction and by instructional information.

EXAMPLE 7.12   DIRECT AND INDIRECT INSTRUCTIONS AND
INSTRUCTIONAL INFORMATION IN ONE TEXT

> *Section 2–19*
> The 382A calibrator may be used to regulate the voltage of another power supply having higher output voltage, but poorer regulation, than the 382A. This is performed as follows:
>
> 1. Connect the 382A and the other power supply at the + and − sens and out terminals. The diode limits the voltage of a reverse polarity which would be applied to the 382A in the event of a short circuit across the load, or when the other instrument is turned on first.
> 2. The rating of the fuse should be equal to, or slightly higher than, the rated full load current of the other power supply. The fuse is a protective device which opens the circuit if the load becomes shorted, to prevent applying a continuing reverse voltage to the 382A.
> 3. Install a diode capable of conducting the maximum short circuit current of the other power supply until the fuse opens the circuit.
> 4. The resistor is an external voltage control resistor, the value of

which must be 1000 ohms per volt of the output of the other
power supply.

[Source: *Operator's Manual*, Fluke Manufacturing Co., p. 4-10.]

[This set of instructions mixes direct and indirect instructions and
instructional information in the following way:

The introduction gives us the purpose (goal) of the set of
instructions.

Instruction 1 begins with a direct instruction (marked by the use of
the imperative). The second sentence is a piece of instructional
information explaining the purpose of the diode CR1 and adding a
small amount of 'theory'.

Instruction 2 begins with an indirect instruction, marked by the
modal 'should'. The reader familiar with the conventions of written
instructional discourse will read this sentence as though it is a direct
instruction: 'Use a fuse with a rating equal to or slightly higher than
the full rated load current of the other power supply.' The second
sentence is again information, telling readers the purpose of the fuse
and adding a bit more theory.

Instruction 3 is a direct instruction that includes a brief function
description of the diode to be installed.

Instruction 4 reverses the order of instruction 2 by giving us the
instructional information first and then the indirect instruction. Both
pieces of information can be incorporated into a single direct
instruction: 'Use an external voltage control resistor that has the
value of 1000 ohms per volt of the output of the other power supply.'

The type of rephrasing shown above for instructions 2 and 4 can be
the basis for useful student exercises. To rephrase indirect
instructions provides practice in using imperatives; to rephrase direct
instructions provides practice in producing and using modals and, as
later examples show, in producing and using passives and passive
modals. Chapter 8 looks more closely at passives, modals, and
passive models, all of which tend to cause problems for many non-
native learners.

A problem not touched upon to any great extent so far is that of the
specialized vocabulary of this type of discourse, primarily the heavy
use of noun compounds. These are discussed in chapter 9.]

CHART 7.6   INFORMATION GIVEN BY TYPES OF INSTRUCTIONS

  I.   *Instructions*

     1.   Direct instructions. Direct instructions use the imperative form
of the verb. As a rule, they are given in the form of a numbered
list; that is, a set of steps in the order in which they are to be
done.

     2.   Indirect instructions. Indirect instructions use non-imperative
verb forms. The most frequent forms used with indirect

instructions are passive verbs, modals, and passive modals, with this last being extremely common. Indirect instructions are almost always in paragraph, rather than in list, form, with the core statement of the paragraph being the goal (or purpose) of the instructions. When they are in list form, they frequently accompany a direct instruction or some instructional information.

[Direct and indirect instructions are often mixed together. Usually, as noted directly above, they are together in a numbered list; however, when the mixture includes instructional information, each item in the list can become a separate physical paragraph, with the entire set of instructions making up one conceptual paragraph.]

II.   *Instructional information*
By instructional information we mean information that helps the reader make use of or better understand the instructions. Instructional information cannot stand alone but is always associated with either direct or indirect instructions. It is, therefore, adding one or more of the following kinds of information to direct or indirect instructions.
1. Cautions: 'This circuit will short out under any overload.'
2. Warnings (often a kind of negative instruction): 'Do not use the intake duct as a shelf for tools.'
3. Notes: 'Ripple functions to provide a path for AC voltages.'
4. Specifying statements: 'Only manual transmission models have two thermosensors; automatics have only one.'
5. Theory (the 'why' an instruction is to be carried out as specified):
[First, the instruction, in this case a direct instruction:] 'The VRU mounting *must* be a rigid and flat horizontal plate . . .'
[Second, the 'why' of the instruction:] '. . . to avoid introducing errors due to flexing of the mounting plate.'

[It is not always necessary to make distinctions as fine as those made above. This is especially true with intermediate or lower-level classes. With these, we refer to 'cautions and warnings', avoiding making distinctions that are not always easily seen. In the same fashion, 'notes', 'specifying statements', and even 'theory' can be profitably lumped together. With more advanced classes, however, 'theory' is often best left by itself.]

7.5.2   Teaching the rhetoric of instructions

As we shall see from the examples in this sub-section, not all sets of instructions are well written. In fact, many seem to be inadequate in one or more respects: they lack clarity; they contain ambiguities; they often lack organization; they leave new terms undefined; and so on. Here we have a partial answer to those teachers of technical writing (and technical reading) who ask, 'How can we teach "good" writing with examples like these?' Too many teachers attempt to solve the problem by selecting only 'good' examples to present to their students. Unfortunately, these same students will face a great deal of 'less than good' writing in the real world, in fact, may already have faced it in some of their textbooks and supplementary reading. To keep them from exposure to all of the kinds of discourse that they will ultimately face means that they will not be able to fully understand nor make use of these instruments when they need to. While most native students have little trouble reading an indirect instruction as a direct instruction, few non-native students can do so without being taught to make the transformation as they read.

Non-native learners find problems of style as well as those of lexis and syntax to some degree in virtually every technical manual. Outside of dense writing, a style problem that students find difficult to handle is the shift from the very formal to the very colloquial and back again. Example 7.13 illustrates this shift. While the style and tone in this example are exaggeratedly informal in the first paragraph as compared to the second (formal) and the third (a compromise), this kind of shifting is becoming more and more the rule, especially when a supposed 'expert' is writing for a lay audience (for example, hobby and other do-it-yourself instructional materials).

EXAMPLE 7.13   STYLE SHIFT IN ONE TYPE OF INSTRUCTIONAL MANUAL

The battery

You probably take your car's battery pretty much for granted. In fact, you've probably been ignoring if not totally abusing your battery all summer and getting away with it. But unless you want to be walking that first morning winter hits hard, you'd better reestablish a proper relationship with your battery . . .. Cold absolutely zonks a battery.

Specific gravity. A standard storage battery produces current on demand through a chemical reaction between the battery plate material and the sulphuric acid in the electrolyte liquid. When a battery is fully charged there is a high percentage of acid in the electrolyte to react with the plates. Since acid is heavier than water, the specific gravity is high if a battery is in good condition.

Strength test. To check out a battery with a hydrometer, simply draw a sample of electrolyte from each battery cell – jotting down the specific gravity reading . . .. A good cell will have a reading of

1.260 or higher. A discharged cell will read 1.160 or lower based on 80 degrees F.

[Source: *Do-Your-Own Car Repairs* (Washington, D.C., United States Government, n.d.), n.p.]

[By the time an EST class reaches the point where material of this kind is discussed, few students have difficulty reading at the level of paragraph 2 as this is close to the style of their subject-matter reading. They do, however, have considerable problems with the first paragraph or any writing similarly colloquial. Paragraph 3 usually causes problems only for those students whose oral English is still confined to the classroom: thus, they may have difficulty with (in the context of informational writing) such terms as 'check out', 'simply draw . . .', and 'jotting down'. This difficulty disappears as a rule once the students are able to handle language exchanges with native speakers.]

A few of the syntactic and lexical problems that occur all too often in technical manuals are illustrated in example 7.14. Poor organization in instructions is illustrated in section 7.6, example 7.18. Other grammatical problems are discussed in chapter 8; lexical problems in chapter 9; and possible solutions in chapter 10.

EXAMPLE 7.14   SYNTAX AND LEXIS PROBLEMS IN A SET OF INSTRUCTIONS

Technical services repair card

1. Oil tank quantity must be 12 quarts or more.
2. Remove engine oil screen for disposal.
3. Before installing the external filter assembly, check the red button at top of filter. If it raises 3/16 inch, filter element should be changed. P/N 27-7965.
4. Place filter assembly mounted on a cart under each engine screen. Each cart is placarded to be used for specific engine position.
5. The filter assembly P/N AD-83330-24 should be at least full with Mobil Jet Oil II.
6. When servicing the filter assembly, be sure that the valve at the bottom of the filter is in close position.
7. The inlet and outlet port of the filter assembly are attached to a typical screen cover (JT8D) and a false filter inserted.
8. Open valve located at bottom of filter to full open position. Repeat valve should be opened to full open position before starting engine.
9. Run engine at 1.02–1.04 EPR for five minutes and observe oil pressure 40–35 PSIG. Oil temperature maximum 120 degree C. Oil quantity not less than 12 quarts.

10.   After engine shutdown, close valve at bottom of the filter and remove filter assembly cart and install new main oil screen. Assemble screen per MSL 79–005, M.N. 79–90. Torque cover to 25–30 in./lbs. Safety nuts and run engine and check screen for leaks.

11.   Service oil tank.

[Source: *Saudia Technical Repair Manual* (Jeddah, Saudi Arabia, Saudi Arabian Airlines, n.d.), n.p.]

[Of the eleven separate instructions in the example, eight invariably cause trouble for non-native readers. Since almost all of the mechanics using this repair card are non-native speakers living in their home environment, the extent of the problem is obvious. The errors and the difficulties of syntax and lexis are not, however, because the manual was written by a non-native speaker; on the contrary, it is the work of native English-speaking aircraft engineers.

Of the eleven instructions four are indirect and five direct, with two, instructions 3 and 8, mixed. Instruction 10 has five separate direct instructions crammed into four sentences. Instructions 1, 2, and 11 are clear; however, this is not true of the other eight. In instruction 3, we find a final sentence (or symbols set off as a sentence) with no indication of the relation of this to the rest of the instruction until we get to instruction 5, where the symbols suggest that parts numbers beginning with P/N have something to do with filters. Instruction 4 is both ambiguous and confusing: it is difficult to determine from the text whether the filter assembly is to be mounted on a cart or is found already mounted on a cart. The word 'placarded' in the second sentence is little used as a verb and is found only as a noun, if at all, in most of the dictionaries non-native readers use. (By asking trained Saudia mechanics we learned that the instruction means that on each cart there is a filter assembly and that these carts are furnished with placards telling the mechanics what part of the engine the assembly on the cart is designed for.)

Instruction 5 is, of course, simply careless writing. If something is 'at least full', it is 'full'. (Some of the senior technicians discovered their trainees over-filling filter assemblies to make certain that they were actually 'full'!) Instruction 6 caused similar problems of interpretation with some users of the manual interpreting 'close position' as 'fully closed' and others interpreting it as 'near closed position but not necessarily completely closed'. Instruction 7 is a good example of an apparent passive construction not being a passive but a stative. This problem is treated in detail in chapter 8.

The confusion in instruction 8 is caused by the ambiguous phrasing in sentence 1 and the lack of a definite article in sentence 2. A large proportion of readers first read sentence 1 as 'The open valve is located at the bottom of the filter . . ..' When they reach the end of the sentence all native readers and some non-native readers are able to adjust and so read, 'Open the valve which is located at the bottom of the filter to full open position.' The second sentence was taken by many readers to mean 'The repeat valve should be opened . . . .' whereas it actually means, 'Repeat! The valve . . . .'

Instruction 9 is a good example of the kind of 'cryptic' writing too often found in manuals. In addition to the definite articles omitted, the writer leaves out the key terms that could make the compound direct object of the verb 'observe' clear to the reader. The writer here intended to instruct the reader to run the engine at a certain speed for five minutes and then to check the oil pressure to make sure that it is 40–35 PSIG *and* to check the oil temperature to make sure that it is no higher than 120 degrees C. These observations are to be made with the engine containing not less than 12 quarts of oil. In addition to trying to 'save' words, the writer of this instruction is guilty of upside-down organization of his information: the last sentence should clearly have been placed first: 'With the oil quantity not less than 12 quarts, run the engine . . . .'

Instruction 10 is, as are so many instructions in technical manuals, inconsistent in its use of the definite article. (For a detailed discussion of this problem, see chapter 8.) However, the main impediment to understanding here is the non-standard use of two nouns as verbs in the third and fourth sentences. In sentence 3 we have, 'Torque cover to 25–30 in./lbs.' an apparently verbless unit marked off as a complete sentence. In sentence 4 we have, 'Safety nuts . . . .', two apparent nouns in parallel with two verb + noun groups following. Logic tells us that in these two cases our apparent nouns 'torque' and 'safety' must actually be imperative verb forms. Thus we can read, 'Tighten with the torque wrench until its gage registers between 25–30 in./lbs.' and 'Tighten the nuts to a safe tightness.'

In chapters 8 and 9 additional grammatical and lexical problems are exemplified and discussed. Chapter 10 offers suggestions for coping with these and with the problems pointed out in this chapter.]

7.6 The rhetoric of visual–verbal relationships

By visual–verbal we mean the relationships between visual aids such as drawings, schematics, graphs, tables, charts – any illustrative material – and a piece of text. The function of visual aids is to add information to that given by the discourse; as a result, we find visual aids only in conjunction with other rhetorical features. Whatever the type of visual aid or of rhetorical function and/or rhetorical technique used, the relationships between them (that is, the statements made by the text) should be such that they provide the reader with the following information:[2]
1. When the reader should look at the visual.
2. Where the reader should look for the visual.

3. What the reader should look for in the visual.
4. Why the reader should look at the visual.
These are discussed in more detail in chart 7.7 below.

7.6.1   *Examples of types of visual–verbal relationships*

There are many types of visual aids and each has its own kind of information for the reader. However, all have one characteristic in common: providing information, usually detail, that is tedious to read in solid text, or is difficult or impossible to describe accurately in words alone.

Some of the more common types of visuals found in scientific and technical discourse are tables, graphs, schematics, flow charts, exploded views, maps, photographs, and representative drawings (sometimes to scale). All of these provide us with detail difficult to describe in words. Tables and graphs usually give us numerical detail, with graphs being less precise than tables as they are designed to show relationships quickly and, often, more generally. Schematics and flow charts give similar information to the reader, with the flow chart also showing the stages of a process or a procedure. Exploded views are a kind of visual physical description as they give the spatial relationships of the parts of an object or a device. Maps also show physical relationships but more often of territory than of machinery, although we do find maps that show, for example, the positions of the various pieces of machinery on a factory floor. Photographs cover a wide range of types of information – from blown-up fine detail, such as textures, to great sweeps of land. Representative drawings, especially those drawn to scale, are like exploded views in that they also give us a visualization of physical description and space order. However, without some kind of text explanation, no type of visual provides information with the same clarity and precision that well-written scientific and technical discourse does.

Whatever the nature of the visual, the text should provide at a minimum the information listed above in section 7.6. Chart 7.7 expands on this list.

CHART 7.7   VISUAL–VERBAL RELATIONSHIPS: TEXT
INFORMATION

The text accompanying a visual should answer – as a minimum – the following questions:
1. When should readers look at the visual? Should they look at first mention of the visual? During the reading? After the reading?
2. Where should readers look for the visual? (This information is usually given when the location of the visual is not apparent to the reader.)

3. What should readers look for in the visual? What are the focal points? (The accompanying text should make these clear.)
4. Why should readers look at the visual? What are the meaningful relationships between the visual and the accompanying text and between the visual, the accompanying text, and the subject matter of the total discourse?

A major problem in visual–verbal relationships is suggested by point 2 above. Where should visuals be placed in relation to their text so that they are most useful to the reader? In their efforts to answer this question, most scientific and technical writers seem to apply the 'rules' given in chart 7.8.

CHART 7.8 'RULES' FOR PLACEMENT OF VISUALS

1. If the visual is of direct importance to the discourse:
   a) Put the visual on the page with its text – if the visual is small enough to fit on the page (that is, if the visual is one-third of a page or less in size).
   b) Put the visual on the following page – if the visual is too large (over half a page) to go on the page with its text.
   c) Put visuals at the end of the text (or at the end of a chapter or section) – if there are several related visuals and they cannot be put on the page with their texts or on the following page(s).

2. If the visual is not of direct importance to the discourse, put it (them) at the end of the total discourse or in a position that does not appear to give it more importance than it warrants.

A factor in the relationship of visuals and verbals (and while more directly applicable to the writer than the reader, still of use to the latter) is the question of which came first, the visual or the verbal? As a general rule certain types of texts determine their visuals and certain types of visuals determine their texts. However, writers often fail to take advantage of the relationship between the verbal and the visual and instead of letting them complement one another, on the one hand put too much detail in the text and on the other put too much detail in the visual. When text determines visual and when visual determines text is summarized below in chart 7.9.

CHART 7.9 INTERRELATIONSHIPS OF TEXTS AND VISUALS

1. When the type of visual is determined by the text information, there may be illustrations of:
   a) a device or object being described
   b) a process by a flow chart or a schematic
   c) a device or object being defined, usually by a drawing or exploded view, or a definition diagram
   d) the parts of a classification by a classification diagram

e) aids to carrying out instructions by exploded views, drawings of parts, circuit diagrams, etc.

f) information difficult to describe in words – texture of materials, complicated schematics and diagrams such as blueprints, troubleshooting charts, etc.

2. When the text information is determined by the type of visuals, there may be illustrations of:

a) summary information by graphs, tables

b) locational information by maps

c) tangential information (often barely mentioned in the text)

Examples 7.15 through 7.18 illustrate different kinds of visuals and/or the different rhetorical elements in the texts related to these visuals. Where the actual relationship in terms of location of visual and text differs from their respective locations in the example, this is noted.

EXAMPLE 7.15   TEXT ILLUSTRATING SEVERAL RHETORICAL PROCESSES

Anchor windlasses

Anchor windlasses are installed on ships primarily for handling and securing anchor and chain used for anchoring ships. In addition, most windlasses are provided with capstans or gypsy heads for handling line and for mooring and warping operations.

Windlasses are located in the bow of the ship for handling the bow anchors.

Landing ships capable of beaching and retracting from the beach area are provided with a separate anchor winch to handle the stern anchor used during these operations.

Anchor windlasses are designed to meet specified conditions as follows:

a) Hoist the anchor and chain from 60 fathoms depth at specified speed.

b) Hoist anchor and chain from 100 fathoms at no specified speed.

c) Stop and hold the anchor and chain by means of the wildcat brake.

d) Develop a specified rope speed on the capstan or gypsy head.

e) Withstand a static load on the capstan or gypsy head equal to the minimum breaking strength of the specified size of rope.

Types

Two general types of windlasses are installed on naval ships. These are the horizontal shaft type and the vertical shaft type. These types are subdivided into classes depending on the power source. These classes include the following:

a) Electric hydraulic drive   c) Steam drive

b) Electric drive   d) Hand drive

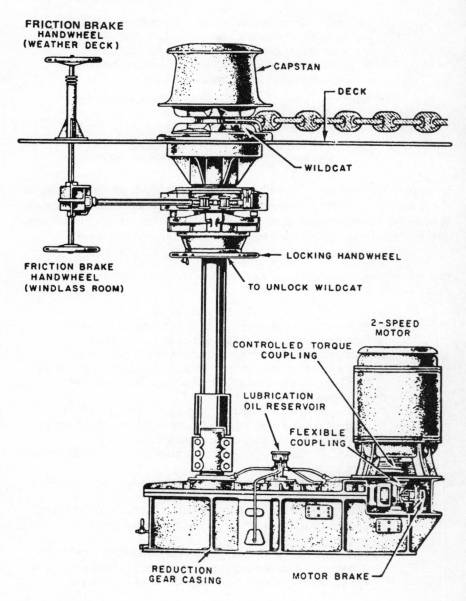

FRICTION BRAKE
HANDWHEEL
(WEATHER DECK)

CAPSTAN

DECK

WILDCAT

FRICTION BRAKE
HANDWHEEL
(WINDLASS ROOM)

LOCKING HANDWHEEL

TO UNLOCK WILDCAT

2-SPEED
MOTOR

CONTROLLED TORQUE
COUPLING

LUBRICATION
OIL RESERVOIR

FLEXIBLE
COUPLING

REDUCTION
GEAR CASING

MOTOR BRAKE

Figure 7.15 Anchor windlass

The essential parts of the windlass, regardless of type and class, are the prime mover, gear transmission, chain wildcat and brake, head for handling line and control means.

Horizontal shaft windlasses are usually made of a self-contained unit with the windlass and the prime mover mounted on the same bedplate.

Vertical shaft windlasses have the power source located below deck with only the wildcat and heads showing above the deck.

Electric hydraulic windlasses
Electric hydraulic windlasses are installed on ships having alternating current supply . . . . [The remainder of the text continues the discussion of 'types of anchor windlasses' by describing each of the four types listed.]

[Source: *Electrician's Mate 3 and 2* (Bureau of Naval Personnel, NAVPERS 10546-A, 1964), p. 328.]

[This selection, from a United States Navy training manual, contains 1. function description – the statement of purposes in the paragraph beginning 'Anchor windlasses are designed to meet specified conditions as follows'; 2. physical description – scattered in several places; 3. partition – following the list of members of the class; 4. semi-formal definitions (but with the class 'windlasses' clearly understood) of horizontal and vertical shaft windlasses – in the two paragraphs following the paragraph of partition; and 5. two levels of classification: the first level has the class 'windlasses', with the members differentiated by type into 'horizontal' and 'vertical'; and the second level has two classes, which are the members of the first level, each having four members with the same names and each having the same basis for differences, 'power source'. The reference to the visual is with the remaining text.

In the original, the visual shown here below is on the page following the above part of the text. The remainder of the text is beneath the visual, which by itself takes up over half of the page (thus breaking rules 1 and 2 of the 'Rules for placement' (chart 7.8). Note that the visual contains more information than is given in the text. (The part of the text not given above has no references to any of the terms shown as labels on the visual.) This is a good example of how a visual can add information to a text and can also make the information that is in the text easier to understand.]

Example 7.16 is from the same training manual. Its visual differs from that of the anchor windlass in that it attempts to illustrate an activity occurring in an object rather than just the object itself. In the original the visual takes up just under one-third of the page but is on the page following that part of the text quoted in the example because of the requirements of page layout, in itself a frequent problem for technical writers.

EXAMPLE 7.16   TEXT CONTAINING MOSTLY INSTRUCTIONAL
INFORMATION

The magnetic blowout operation is illustrated in fig. 7.16. It is
important that the fluxes remain in the proper relationships.
Otherwise, if the direction of the current is changed, the blowout
flux will be reversed and the arc will actually be pulled into the
space between the contacts.

When the direction of electron flow and flux are as illustrated in
fig. 7.16, the blowout force is upward. The blowout effect varies
with the magnitude of the current and with the blowout flux. The
blowout coil should be chosen so that the correct amount of flux
will be obtained. The blowout flux across the arc gap is
concentrated by a magnetic path provided by the steel core in the
blowout coil and the steel pole pieces extending from the core to
either side of the gap.

[Source: *Electrician's Mate 3 and 2*, pp. 206–7.]

[The text is a mixture of indirect instruction ('The blowout coil
should be chosen . . . .') and instructional information (remainder of
the text) plus a small amount of physical description ('. . . provided
by the steel core in the blowout coil and the steel pole pieces
extending from the core to either side of the gap'). The visual, as
noted above, is a kind of function description of the desired activity.]

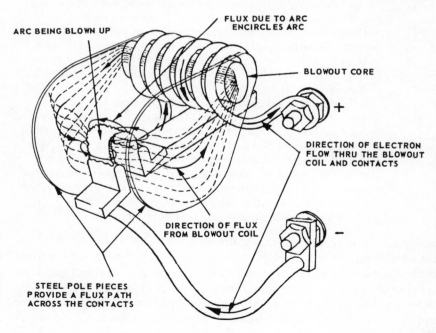

Figure 7.16   Action of magnetic blowout

[The visual for example 7.16 clarifies a function description rather difficult to put into words, thus enabling readers to grasp the problem of arc caused melt and its solution by magnetic blowout.]

EXAMPLE 7.17   TEXT SHOWING TIME PROCESS IN A SET OF INSTRUCTIONS

Carriage removal and disassembly

1. Remove the snap rings from the chain anchors and pull the chain anchors out of the carriage.
2. Secure the carriage with an overhead crane. Remove the carriage by pulling it out of the bottom of the mast channels.
3. Remove the two middle and two lower assemblies.
4. Remove the two upper roller assemblies by removing the cap-screws that connect the retaining plates to the stub shafts. Pull the roller assemblies off the stub shafts.

[Source: *Quad Lift Mast Service Manual*, p. 22. (This is the same text as example 6.2B, p. 56 above.)]

[This is an example of 'good' instruction writing: each instruction is clearly separated from the others; each is written in the same 'style'; the articles are not omitted as is so often the case in sets of instructions; and the steps are given in the order to be followed (not always the case in instructions – see example 7.18). The visual (shown below) is on the same page as the text. It provides us with a type of 'visual' partition (almost an exploded view) that not only shows each part mentioned in the set of instructions but shows also the spatial relationships of those parts to one another.]

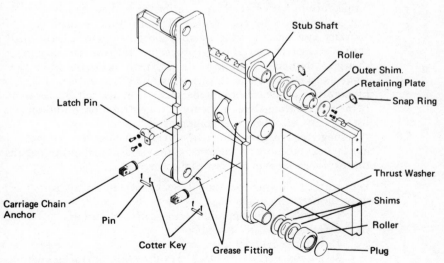

Figure 7.17 Carriage

Example 7.18 is a 'negative' example in that it illustrates how the organization of a set of instructions can cause confusion or, at the very least, slow response on the part of the user. The visual is not shown but is described in the commentary following the example.

EXAMPLE 7.18   TEXT ILLUSTRATING AN AWKWARDLY
ORGANIZED SET OF INSTRUCTIONS

Operating instructions for underwater breathing apparatus
Perform the following operational checks and adjustments prior to using the breathing apparatus.
a. Lay the breathing apparatus on a clean work surface.
b. Remove canister assembly (7) from back plate (18) by removing cylinder spreader bar (24), disconnecting control block to canister hose (15) at air inlet block (16), and unthreading hoses (25 and 26) from breathing bag and vest assembly (17).
c. Remove regulator assembly (13) and control block assembly (14) from the back plate by disconnecting pull rod (27) and loosening regulator yoke assembly (22).

[Source: 'Section IV', *Service Manual for Mark VI Underwater Breathing Apparatus*, Navships 393–0653 (Washington, D.C., Bureau of Ships, U.S. Department of the Navy, 1963), p. 4–1; quoted in Thomas E. Pearsall, *Audience Analysis for Technical Writing* (Beverly Hills, California: Glencoe Press, 1969), p. 43.]

[The visual for this text (a kind of exploded view of the apparatus) is in section 2 and the reader is sent back to this section. As the set of instructions is accompanied by numbers that refer to numbers on the visual, turning back several times during the reading of each instruction makes this arrangement of information less than satisfactory. Concerning the organization, the steps to be performed start in each of the two groups of procedures with the last step and then go to the first step and work through to the next to last step. The students asked to evaluate this set of instructions found the organization awkward and cumbersome. They also felt that the steps of the process would be easier to follow put in the more traditional list form instead of being in paragraphs.

A suggested reorganization that covers both the organizational and layout objections and also brings the visual onto the same page as the text for easier reference is the following:

Perform the following operational checks and adjustments prior to using the breathing apparatus.
I.   Lay the breathing apparatus on a clean work surface.
II. To remove canister assembly:
  1. Remove cylinder spreader bar (24).
  2. Disconnect control block to canister hose (15) at air inlet block (16).

    3. Unthread hoses (25 and 26) from breathing bag and vest assembly (27).
    4. Remove canister assembly (7) from back plate (18).
III.   To remove regulator and control block assemblies:
    1. Disconnect pull rod (27).
    2. Loosen regulator yoke assembly (22).
    3. Remove regulator assembly (13) from the back plate.
    4. Remove control block assembly (14) from the back plate.

The 'use and non-use' of definite articles have followed the pattern of the original version: except for the definite articles preceding 'back plate' in section c in the original and in section III, 3 and 4 in the revision, the writer has chosen not to use any. This inconsistent use of the definite article is common in instructional writing. Why writers will use an article in front of one noun and not another or in front of a noun in one position and not in front of the same noun in another position is one of the unsolved mysteries of written EST discourse. Several theories have been advanced but only in relation to specific texts; no generalizations that appear to hold in all cases have yet been put forward. This problem of the inconsistent use (or lack of use) of the definite article is discussed in detail in chapter 8.]

Examples 7.19 and 7.20 differ markedly from those above as well as from one another. Example 7.19 is from a book explaining physics to the lay reader and so is akin to an instructional text, while example 7.20 is from a repair manual for the Boeing 737 aircraft.

EXAMPLE 7.19   VISUAL WITH TEXT AN EXPANSION OF THE CAPTION

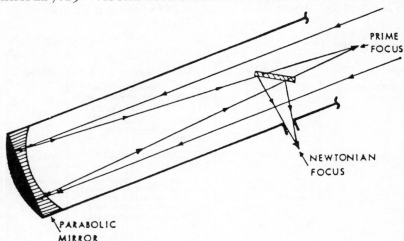

Fig. 7.19 A simplified diagram of a reflector telescope. Starlight is collected and reflected without aberration by a parabolic mirror at

the bottom of a long tube, and focused at some point along the tube's length. A small mirror suspended within the tube reflects focused image through an eyepiece at the side of the tube. Small suspended mirror does not interfere significantly with light-gathering by the large parabolic mirror.

[Source: Alan E. Nourse, M.D., *Universe, Earth, and Atom: the Story of Physics* *(New York: Harper and Row, 1969), p. 380.]*

[The text following the caption is not a paragraph, despite its physical form. The first two sentences following the caption are process description; the third sentence simply adds information on the function of one part of the apparatus. Note also that the writer leaves out some of the definite articles beginning with the second sentence; he is not, however, consistent when he shifts to this 'note' style. Additional information relating to the visual is in two paragraphs on the preceding page. This type of arrangement with the main text discussing the question 'Why should the reader look at the visual?' and the question 'What should the reader look for?' answered by that part of the text under the visual and following the caption is common in textbooks and related reading material.]

Example 7.20 is a troubleshooting chart containing more information than the average. Troubleshooting charts as a rule have three columns; this example has four, with column 3 the one that is usually left out. Most troubleshooting charts have columns labelled 'Problem', 'Cause' and 'Solution' (or words with similar meanings).

EXAMPLE 7.20   VISUAL AND TEXT AS AN INDIVISIBLE UNIT

Procedure 48

Symptom	Probable cause	Isolation procedure	Remedy
OVERSPEED automatic shutdown.		Turn APU master switch OFF and momentarily press overspeed reset switch on APU control unit.	
		Start APU and listen for noise or vibration and check for oil in exhaust.	
	Fuel control unit defective.	If APU starts and overspeeds, replace fuel control unit.	Replace fuel control unit.
	Centrifugal switch assembly/electronic speed switch or APU control unit defective.	If APU starts but does not overspeed and OVERSPEED light comes on, replace centrifugal switch assembly/electronic speed switch. If problem persists, replace APU control unit.	Replace defective component.

[Source: Technical Publications Department, *737 APU Troubleshooting Guide* (Phoenix, Arizona, The Garrett Corporation, n.d.), p. 110.]

[The text and the visual are the same in this type of discourse: the visual is a kind of matrix with (in this case) four vertical columns and the number of horizontal rows determined by the number of 'symptoms' in a given chart.]

Working with visuals and visual–verbal relationships in the classroom is discussed in chapter 10, where several exercises in producing both texts and visuals are treated in some detail.

In chapter 8 we look at the troublesome grammatical problems that occur with certain rhetorical features, with the majority of these problems occurring with the rhetoric of instructions. In chapter 9 we examine two problems in lexis, both found in conjunction with all of the rhetorical features treated in this book. Chapter 10 suggests ways in which the rhetorical, grammatical, and lexical problems can be attacked in the EST classroom.

8 Rhetorical–grammatical relationships

8.1 Introduction

Up to this point the analysis process has been applied to the paragraph, the rhetorical techniques and the rhetorical functions, with only occasional reference to the grammatical problems encountered by the non-native EST student. I am not referring here to the basic grammar of the English language but to those specific grammatical elements that appear to stand in a special relationship with some of the rhetorical concepts that we have been examining.

Our work in the area of rhetorical–grammatical relationships began at almost the same time as our research. In analyzing students' reading performances we discovered that writers of scientific and technical discourse make certain assumptions – which we call presuppositions – concerning the kind and amounts of grammatical–rhetorical information that they assume readers share with them; that is, that readers bring to their EST reading. These assumptions appear to be, for the most part, valid for the native learner, but not for the non-native learner. Our research showed – and continues to show – that the majority of non-native students lack the cultural background that enables them to bring more than a very limited amount of the presupposed information to their reading of EST discourse.

Out of this same research has grown the realization that the number of ways in which the grammatical elements involved with the rhetoric can be expressed is not just a matter of choice on the part of the writer. Further exploration of this idea has resulted in the following conclusions:

1. The expression of the grammatical elements that are very frequently coupled with specific rhetorical features is sufficiently patterned to allow us to make generalizations concerning the relationships between these grammatical elements and the specific rhetorical features.
2. Part of the presuppositional information that a native student brings to reading EST discourse is the ability to comprehend these grammatical elements without special training. The same is not true, however, for the majority of non-native students.
3. Thus, we conclude that a good deal of the ability of a reader to handle the presuppositional factors in written EST discourse is a function of

the relationship between the language and those socio-cultural elements associated with it.

4. The rhetorical functions most affected by the grammar are those that writers choose most frequently to transmit much of the basic scientific and technical information on which they base a given technical piece of discourse.

The areas of rhetoric most involved with the more difficult grammatical elements are 1. description; 2. instructions; and 3. a very narrow area in the field of 'peer writing'. This area we call 'the rhetoric of background information': we find it in sections of scientific articles, books, reports, dissertations, theses, etc. in which it is necessary for writers to report on the work of others in the same field of research, especially that most affecting the writers' own work.

The grammatical elements that cause the most difficulty are 1. passive–stative distinctions in the rhetoric of description and of instructions; 2. modal use in the rhetoric of instructions; 3. non-standard use (and non-use) of the definite article in the rhetoric of description and of instructions; and 4. tense choice in the rhetoric of description and of background information, this choice depending on what we call 'non-temporal' factors. Each of these problems is taken up in detail below.

8.2 Passive–stative distinctions

Both passive and stative verbs are found primarily in the rhetoric of description; we find them also in the rhetoric of instructions but less frequently. By stative we mean those constructions that on the surface resemble passives in that they consist of the verb 'to be' plus a past participle. (We are not concerned here with those verbs that are inherently stative such as 'weigh', 'have' – meaning 'possess' – etc.) Example 8.1 illustrates passive and stative forms that are similar in appearance but distinctly different in meaning and in function.

EXAMPLE 8.1   SIMILARITIES AND DIFFERENCES IN PASSIVE AND STATIVE VERB FORMS

> *Passives*
> 'The heat exchanger assembly *is lowered* from the compartment while resting on the platform. The platform *is lowered* and *raised* by the hoist crank.'
>
> *Statives*
> 'The RS-5 system *is composed of* an undersea acoustic beacon, a surface-vessel mounted array ... a vertical reference unit ... [and]

115

control unit. The sensor *is housed* in a support assembly. . . . When the gear *is down* and *locked*. . . .'

[Sources: Passive, quoted in a student report; precise source unknown. Stative, *Honeywell Acoustic Position Indicator RS-5 Operation and Maintenance Manual*, vols. I and II (Seattle, Honeywell Marine Systems Center, 1970), p. 1–4.]

[The passive paragraph contains three passives, one without an agent (sentence 1) and two with an agent (sentence 2). The stative paragraph also has three 'to be + past participle' structures, each appearing to be an agentless passive. The difference between agentless passives and statives can be seen by the contrasting examples in the two paragraphs: in the 'passive' paragraph, *first lowered* is in a context that clearly marks it as an activity. In the 'stative' paragraph, *is down and [is] locked* are both clearly descriptive in their context – the first being the 'real' adjective; the second, the participle.]

In other words, a passive always indicates an activity (despite its name) whether or not it has a stated agent to perform that activity; a stative, in contrast, always describes the state or condition of the grammatical subject of the sentence the stative verb is in. A stative, then, is simply one type of adjective–verb phrase. In 'The door is open' we have verb + adjective. In 'The door is closed' we also have verb + adjective but with the adjective a past participle.

When non-native students are faced with a stative the problem is almost invariably one of misidentification. They assume, not without a certain logic, that any form of 'to be + past participle' is a passive. (Even native speakers can have trouble sorting out the grammatical difference between the forms of 'was locked' in 'The door to the garden was locked' and 'The door to the garden was locked at night by the gardener.') The initial move of non-native students when faced with statives is to attempt to turn them into active verb phrases. Since statives appear to be agentless passives, these students resort to the 'rules' laid down for transforming agentless passive sentences into active ones and make a subject for the active verb by using 'someone' or 'something'. Thus, the stative 'When the gear is down and locked . . .' becomes 'When someone locked the gear down . . .' and 'The sensor is housed . . .' becomes 'Someone housed the sensor . . .', neither of which is the meaning intended by the stative structures.

In our work we find the assumption that 'to be + past participle' statives are agentless passives and thus can be transformed into actives most frequent in those students whose languages do not have an identifiable equivalent to the English passive. Their tendency is usually to 'over-learn' how to handle passive structures with the result that any 'to be +

past participle' is transformed into an active structure and then into the native language.

An even more difficult type of discourse for the non-native student is the text that mixes passives and statives. This is often the case with paragraphs of description since many mix physical description – which uses statives – and function and process description – both of which use passives. Example 7.1 is repeated here (numbered as example 8.2) with the passive verb forms in italics and the statives in capital letters.

EXAMPLE 8.2   A PARAGRAPH WITH A MIXTURE OF PASSIVES
AND STATIVES

> A canal bottom sampler, used in Imperial Valley, California, canals, consisted of a brass tube 2.7 centimeters in diameter and 15.2 centimeters long. At the bottom WAS ATTACHED a sharp steel cutting blade. The upper end of the tube WAS THREADED into the base of a cone, the shoulder of which prevented the brass tube from sinking into the canal bed beyond the required depth. The upper end of the cone WAS ATTACHED to a handle of $2\frac{1}{2}$-inch pipe, [which WAS] MADE UP OF short sections [which WERE] COUPLED together so that the length of the handle *could be varied* according to the depth of the water. In taking a sample, the tube *was pushed* into the bottom deposit as far as the shoulder of the cone permitted. The handle *was filled* with water and a cap *was screwed* on the upper end. When the tube *was withdrawn* a partial vacuum *was formed*, which held the sample in the tube.

> [The five stative verbs are all part of the physical description while the five passive verbs are all used with function description (the first passive) and with process description (the four remaining passives). On first reading it might seem that such forms as 'was attached' and 'was threaded' are passive, but a closer reading shows that the writer is not describing activities but the conditions that resulted from them.]

Chart 8.1 summarizes the passive–stative distinctions discussed and illustrated above. From both students and teachers we have learned that the chart is best used as a reference, especially for those readers whose languages do not contain passives as we conceive them.

CHART 8.1   SUMMARY OF TYPES OF INFORMATION FROM
PASSIVE AND STATIVE CONSTRUCTIONS

> Passives
> There are two types of passive constructions: those with an agent stated and those without an agent stated.

A passive with an agent provides readers with the following information:

1. the grammatical subject of the sentence (the nominative form usually preceding the verb and related to it by being the receiver of the action indicated by that verb);
2. the tense (and thus usually the time) as well as the mood of the verb.
3. the agent – the performer of the action indicated by the verb and the 'true' as well as the grammatical subject of the verb when it is transformed into its active form.

Using this information, we can transform the passive sentence into an active one by the following process:

Step 1. Place the agent before the verb.

Step 2. Change the verb to its active form, keeping the tense and mood of the passive.

Step 3. Place the grammatical subject of the passive sentence after the verb, thus giving it the standard position of a direct object, which it has become.

A passive without an agent provides readers with the information given above in 1 and 2. As this type of passive has a grammatical but not a 'true' subject, one must be provided when a transformation to the active is made. If no other subject is indicated by the context, 'someone' or 'something' – whichever is the more logical – is most often used when making step 1 of the transformation process. Steps 2 and 3 are the same as when making a transformation with a passive with agent.

Statives

There are several types of stative constructions; however, only the one that looks like a passive without an agent concerns us here.

Statives provide readers with the following information:

1. a word or phrase that is both the grammatical and the 'true' subject of the verb;
2. a copulative verb (almost always a form of 'to be') that gives us the tense – and thus often the time – of the verb;
3. a word or phrase functioning as an adjective, this word or phrase having as its center a past participal form.

Although the above elements look the same as those found in an agentless passive, they function differently – as their definitions make clear. Therefore, while it is possible to transform a stative sentence into an active one, the result is neither logical nor semantically acceptable as it does not provide the information the writer intended. For example, in the stative sentence 'The sensor is housed in a support assembly', a transformation to the passive would give us 'Someone houses (or housed) the sensor in a support assembly.' This would be a statement of an activity; the writer, however, is not describing an activity but giving a physical (and therefore static) description of *the result of an activity*.

118

8.3   Modal use in the rhetoric of instructions

Modals, especially passive modals, are found commonly in scientific and technical discourse, especially in peer writing (the left end of the 'Spectrum', p. 6) in such phrases as 'It should be made clear that. . . .', 'It can be assumed that. . . . .', etc. Our concern here, however, is not with this kind of semi-jargon but with the modal forms that shift from their 'standard' meanings when used in instructions and related discourse. As a rule, we find this meaning shift with the modal 'should' and less commonly with 'can' and 'may'. By 'meaning shift' here I mean that the commonly taught meanings for 'should' – and sometimes 'can' and 'may' – do not fit the context of the discourse (nor the intent of the writer).

In what we might call 'general English' oriented grammars, the consensus seems to be that 'should' and 'ought to' have a meaning close to 'must' – in the sense of obligation – but with less force, less insistence that something be done (or not be done).[1] Only a few of the books on scientific English comment on these modals and then to a very limited degree – perhaps because they seldom deal directly with the discourse of occupational English.[2] Two books, however, do point out that in certain instances 'should' has the force of 'must': in their work on scientific and technical English for non-native speakers, Huckin and Olsen use graphics to show the relationship of 'must' and 'should' in respect to degrees of obligation and of probability.[3] Leech and Svartvik, although not specifically concerned with the English of science and technology, briefly discuss the meaning of 'should' (and 'ought to') in commands and instructions: 'Strictly, these leave the decision about what to do in the hands of the hearer. But in practice, as the examples show, they are often tactful ways of giving commands or instructions.'[4]

It is in this sense that we find the most common use of 'should' in the rhetoric of instructions, usually when the reader is being warned to do or not to do something. Example 8.4, from an instructional manual on welding, shows both 'should' and 'may' used in the sense of 'must' in the paragraphs under the heading 'Weld backing'. In contrast, the paragraph labeled 'Edge preparation' has 'must' rather than 'should' with the meaning of 'must' and it also uses 'may' in its more standard use. The three modals in this paragraph of the example – 'must', 'may', and 'can' – are also passives. Thus we have three passive modals, illustrating a typical structure found in indirect instructions in occupational English discourse. The 'non-standard' uses of 'should' and 'may' as well as the passive modals are shown by italics.

119

EXAMPLE 8.3   NON-STANDARD USES OF *SHOULD* AND *MAY*
AND PASSIVE MODALS IN A SET OF INDIRECT INSTRUCTIONS

Weld backing

Steel weld backing *should be* sufficiently thick so that the molten metal will not burn through the backing. In most cases the steel weld backing is fused and remains part of the weldment.

One of the best possible nonfusible weld backings is copper. Copper *should be* of a sufficient mass or liquid cooled so as to readily dissipate the heat. For steel thicknesses other than gage material, a relief groove *may be* necessary. The depth of this relief groove *may be* as little as 0.02″ or as much as 1/8″ or more.

Edge preparation

Particularly for heavier weld sections the edges of the metal *must be prepared* for submerged arc welding. Various methods *may be employed* in preparing the edges for welding.... Metal cutting or grooving *can* also *be accomplished* by the carbon-arc method.

[Source: *Submerged Arc Welding: Processes and Applications* (Hobart Technical Center, n.d.), n.p.]

['Should' clearly means 'must' in the first sentence under the heading 'Weld backing'. The writer is saying in effect, 'If the steel weld backing is not sufficiently thick, the molten metal will burn through the backing.' The second example is much the same: 'If the copper is not of sufficient mass or liquid cooled it will not readily dissipate the heat; therefore it *must* be of a sufficient mass.....' 'May', is usually a bit more difficult to read as 'must' here. However, a close examination shows that it is not a matter of choice on the part of the welder to make a relief groove should the steel have a thickness other than gage. If so, the groove *must be* made; the only choice is one of the depth of that groove. (This information came from a welding instructor.)]

In our experience non-native students tend to transfer their reading techniques developed for 'general English' to reading EST discourse without realizing that adjustments are often necessary. As a result, they read 'should' with the meaning found most commonly in ESL/EFL grammars and so assume that a choice is possible. The student who brought the welding example was puzzled because he had learned to weld and felt that the text was misleading by suggesting that the welder had a choice of procedures. Although he had learned to read instruction manuals (before entering university) he had not learned the differences between 'general English' and EST discourse. This problem is discussed further in chapter 10, where a suggestion for treating it in the classroom is given.

8.4   Problems with the definite article[5]

In addition to the trouble that virtually all non-native learners have with both English articles, EST discourse presents two additional problems with the definite article. The first is inconsistency in the use of the article in the rhetoric of instructions, especially with those sets of instructions found in technical manuals and related material. The second we have called the 'specialized use' of the definite article. This use is found in the rhetoric of description, most often when the functioning of a piece of machinery is being described.

Example 8.4 illustrates the inconsistent use of the definite article in a set of instructions. The writer had twenty-six opportunities to use the definite article as a native speaker would expect it to be used. He did use it 'correctly' in five instances, but ignored it altogether in the remaining twenty-one. This is not an isolated example, as a random look at sets of instructions will show. (See, for instance, example 7.14, p. 100, which includes the inconsistent use of the definite article among its many sins.) In the example below, the five definite articles used are shown in italics; the position of each 'missing' article is shown by the symbol ◇.

EXAMPLE 8.4   INCONSISTENT USE OF THE DEFINITE ARTICLE
IN A SET OF INSTRUCTIONS

Rubber plug method of tubeless tire repair
1. Remove ◇ puncturing object if still in *the* tire (◇ Tire is not dismounted from *the* rim.)
2. Fill ◇ tire with air to 30 psi. Dip ◇ probe into ◇ cement, insert it into ◇ injury and work up and down to lubricate ◇ injury.
3. Grasp each end of ◇ patch. Stretch and roll center of ◇ patch into ◇ eye of ◇ needle. Remove ◇ protective covering from both sides of *the* patch, being careful not to touch ◇ raw rubber.
4. Dip ◇ perma strip into ◇ cement, making sure that all surfaces are coated.
5. Insert ◇ patch slowly and steadily into ◇ injury, up to ◇ handle. Then turn ◇ needle ¼ turn and remove.
6. Without stretching *the* patch, cut it 1/8″ from *the* tread.
7. Inflate to ◇ proper pressure. ◇ Tire is now ready for service.

[Source: Bricker, *Automobile Guide*, p. 467.]

A native reader of EST discourse has little trouble in supplying the missing articles when they are needed to clarify the text. Non-native readers, however, do not have this same 'feel' for the article and so cannot bring to the reading the ability of the native reader. When faced with inconsistencies such as those illustrated above, they tend to apply their 'rote-learned' rules. Arbitrary violation of these rules creates special problems for non-native learners when they attempt to grasp the total meaning of a piece of discourse, especially the dense discourse so common in EST writing.

The same difficulty occurs when the problem is one of 'specialized use' of the definite article. This specialized use is found in the rhetoric of description in all types of EST discourse, including that of example 8.5, which is from an (unidentified) elementary text. When we analyze the example we can see that the writer has applied a special set of 'article rules' that are contrary to the expectations of non-native speakers; that is, to the 'rules' they have learned.

EXAMPLE 8.5   SPECIALIZED USE OF THE DEFINITE ARTICLE

The gas turbine engine fires continuously. The engine draws air through *the* diffuser and into *the* compressor, raising its temperature. The high pressure air passes into *the* combustion chamber, where it is mixed with a fuel and produces an intense flame. The gas from the combustion chamber is directed through the turbine, where the pressure of the gas decreases and its velocity increases. The turbine drives the compressor. The gas increases in speed as it passes through the exhaust nozzle before it is finally expelled from the turbine. A net force results from the change in momentum of the gases between *the inlet* and *the* exhaust. If a gas turbine is intended to drive an automobile, it must be designed so that as much energy as possible is absorbed by the turbine and transferred to *the* drive shaft.

[Source: Furnished by a student from a textbook used in technical schools; precise source unknown.]

[In sentence 1 the definite article is used in a defining (generalizing) statement although standard usage requires either the plural of the noun with no preceding article ('Gas turbine engines fire continuously') or the indefinite article with a singular noun (representing generalization from a single instance: 'A gas turbine engine fires continuously'). In sentences 2 and 3, the first mention in this text of the nouns 'diffuser', 'compressor', and 'combustion chamber' is indicated by the use of the definite rather than the indefinite article as most 'rules' require. This same use of the definite article to mark first mention of a noun is found also in sentences 6 and 7 with the nouns 'exhaust nozzle', 'inlet', and 'exhaust'.

Insofar as we were able to determine by talking to native post-graduate engineering students, to their instructors, and to professional engineers, they were not concerned whether the article indicated first or later mention of the noun. They all took the use of the definite article in sentences 2,3,6 and 7 to indicate that the machinery being described contained *only one* of whatever part was being marked by that article.

In contrast, a brief exercise given to a group of native-speaker candidates for MA degrees in teaching English as a second/foreign language (none of whom had a science background) gave quite different results. The exercise consisted of the above text with all articles replaced by blanks which were to be filled in with either the definite or indefinite article (not with a demonstrative). Of the twenty-four who did the exercise, twenty-two put the indefinite article in the blanks before the nouns in question; the remaining two put both the definite and indefinite articles in each problem blank. It occurred to only a few who did the exercise that the definite article might mark the part being described as 'one of a kind'.]

Non-native readers also try to apply the rules – sometimes with unsatisfactory results, both for reader and writer (not to mention the teacher!). A typical reaction from non-native readers is seen in this remark from a postgraduate student studying electrical engineering: 'I learned the use of articles by remembering the rules. When I read, if the rules do not fit, I ignore the articles. Sometimes that makes more sense to me.' Unfortunately, this way of 'reading' articles appears to hold for many non-native students. While some native readers can bring to their reading information that the writer presupposes they already possess, non-native readers have no such reservoir to draw from. As a result, they either by-pass the problem by ignoring the article altogether or they spend time fruitlessly trying to reconcile an unfamiliar article use with the 'rules' they have so carefully learned. In either case they fail to get the total meaning of the discourse.

8.5 Non-temporal use of tense

By non-temporal use of tense we mean that the writers of a piece of discourse do not use time as the major factor governing their choice of verb tenses. While time is, to some degree, a factor in writers' choices of verb forms, it is not always the primary factor, as we can see from the examples in sub-sections 8.5.1, 8.5.2 and 8.5.3 below. The most frequently used illustration of tense and time not always being in agreement is that of the so-called 'present indicative', which, with most verbs, can indicate almost any other time except 'time now'. This is not the same as the phenomenon described here: for example, using the present tense to represent future action is not a choice dependent on rhetorical factors, while the uses we refer to by 'non-temporal' do include the idea of tense choice being dependent on just such factors.

Three areas where the non-temporal use of tense occurs regularly in written EST discourse are 1. when writers describe apparatus, 2. when they make text references to a visual aid, and 3. when they refer to previously published research (including their own) which is related to the subject of their discourse. This last is that 'rhetoric of background information' mentioned in section 8.1 above.

8.5.1 Description of apparatus

Examples of tense choice based primarily on non-temporal factors are easily found in EST discourse. Examples 7.1 and 7.2 in the preceding chapter illustrate tense choice being dependent on a factor other than time: 'The canal bottom sampler', example 7.1, is described in the past tense, while 'The Peterson dredge', example 7.2, is described in the present tense. Yet both of these pieces of apparatus were developed at about the same time, both had much the same function, and both were written about 'after the fact'. That is, their writers were describing something made and used in the past. Why, then, did the writer of 'The canal bottom sampler' choose the past tense and the writer of 'The Peterson dredge' choose the present tense for their discourse? The answer, fortunately, is a simple one: 'The canal bottom sampler' was used for only a short time and then abandoned as a failure; 'The Peterson dredge', in contrast, was a success and was used up to the time it was written about (and may still be in use).

Based on texts of these types, we can come up with a major criterion for determining tense choice in the rhetoric of description: if the object being described is still functioning as a useful device at the time someone writes about it, the writer will use the present tense. If, on the other hand, the object being described is no longer in use, then the writer will use the past tense. From the two brief but representative texts in example 8.6 below we can state a second criterion for determining tense choice in terms of the temporary or permanent nature of whatever is being described.

EXAMPLE 8.6   NON-TEMPORAL USE OF TENSE IN THE
RHETORIC OF DESCRIPTION

> *Temporary apparatus*
> The test section was constructed of a pure copper cylinder 2 ft long, 6 in in id. and 6.25 in in od. Both ends of the cylinder were closed with removable Pyrex glass end plates $\frac{1}{4}$ in thick. A fluid port was located at each end of the cylinder.

> *Permanent apparatus*
> The measurements were made in the sidewall of the one foot wind tunnel. The tunnel is a blowdown-to-atmosphere facility operating over the mach number range 0.2 to 3.5. Mach number in the tunnel is generated by fixed nozzle blocks at supersonic speeds.

> [Sources: University of Washington (Seattle), College of Engineering Research Reports (n.d., n.p.).]

[Both excerpts can be used successfully with advanced elementary students. The first is from a report on an experiment that used the described piece of apparatus and then broke it apart so that the components could be used for a different experiment at a later date. Since it was a temporary device, the writer describes it in the past tense. The second description, the wind tunnel, is of a piece of apparatus considered to be permanent and so is described in the present tense. (If this tunnel is replaced or torn down, descriptions of it then will be in the past tense.)]

8.5.2   Visual aids

When writers discuss visual aids used in their discourse, the act of gathering the data for the illustration and the designing of the visual have already taken place. Thus, as in the case of description, the activities connected with the visual are, in the writer's mind, in the past. As a result, readers are told about gathering the data and designing the visual in the *past* tense. However, when writers discuss the visual itself and its relationship to the subject at hand, they choose the present tense.

One explanation for this tense shift is the writers continue to think of their work in gathering and using the data for the visual as finished and thus to be written about in the past tense, while in telling the reader when to look at the visual (and sometimes where to find it) and in discussing its relationship to the topic at hand, they shift their point of view from themselves to their readers and so relate their discussion to 'now' – to the moment when the reader is reading this particular piece of discourse. If this explanation is a valid one, then there is clearly a strong temporal factor in the writers' choice of tense; however, it has been argued that the dominant factor here is a non-temporal one: the shift in point of view by writers from themselves to their readers. This shift is illustrated in example 8.7.

EXAMPLE 8.7   TENSE CHOICES IN TEXT ACCOMPANYING A VISUAL

The results which are shown in Table V were achieved by developing a new computer program. These results indicate that it is no longer necessary to budget at the 7 per cent rate for repairs.

[Source: submitted by a student; precise source unknown.]

[Although brief, the above example illustrates the shift in tense accompanying a shift in point of view. The first sentence has a present tense verb when referring readers to the visual (not shown here) and then shifts to the past tense when telling how the data for the visual were obtained. In the second sentence, the writer returns to the present tense in telling readers the importance (to their reading) of the visual to the subject matter of the discourse. This example is suitable for students at intermediate levels and above. Although the subject matter and vocabulary are not too difficult for advanced elementary groups, in our experience this area of EST rhetoric is best reserved for students who have reached intermediate level.]

8.5.3   Reference to previous research[6]

This area of tense choice occurs almost exclusively in the types of discourse that require reporting on earlier, related work done by the writer and, more frequently, by others working in the same field. Discourse of this nature is found almost exclusively at the left end of our 'Spectrum', p. 6, in reports of research done in universities and by government and private research and development groups.

From our research we are able to draw the following conclusions: if writers use the past tense in reporting research done previously by themselves or by others then that research is of secondary importance to the current work being reported on. If, on the other hand, the writer uses the present perfect or the present tense, then the research is of more direct and primary importance to the writer's current work. Also, the present tense is often chosen when a discussion follows the initial citing of a reference to their own or the others' research and/or when important generalizations are being expressed. Example 8.8 illustrates the three tenses functioning as noted above.

EXAMPLE 8.8   TENSE SHIFTS IN THE RHETORIC OF
BACKGROUND INFORMATION

> Among the many statistical studies of data from the IGY
> [International Geophysical Year] are some analyses by Davis
> (1962) of the distributions and motions of auroras in Alaska during
> the last sunspot maximum.... From these studies Davis deduced
> that auroral display was essentially a fixed pattern.... In contrast to
> the statistical methods used by Davis are the detailed studies by
> Akosofu and collaborators (1961–1964) of individual auroral
> displays ... they conclude that there is a basic stable system of
> auroral arcs.... The smallest disturbance is represented by the
> formation of rays which Akosofu has shown to be waves or folds in
> a thin sheet of aurora.... On the other hand Elvey (1957) has
> observed the formation of rayed arcs....

[Source: 'Aural Phenomena, Experiments and Theory', *First Lockheed Research Symposium on Space Science* (Stanford University Press; Oxford University Press, 1965), p. 95.]

[We have the past tense 'deduced' in relation to the year, 1962, the present tense 'conclude' and the present perfect 'has shown to be' with the span of years 1961–1964, and the present perfect again with the earliest date given, 1957. According to our conclusions given above, the work of Davis is less directly related to the research being reported on than is the work of Akosofu and his colleagues, and neither is it as important as the work of Elvey, reported some years previously. The use of the present tense ('conclude') with the initial citing of the work of Akosofu and others is followed in the text by a lengthy discussion only part of which is given in the example.]

8.5.4   Application

For the majority of non-native learners working in science or technology or learning to be technicians (at whatever level) it is important that they be made aware of the tense choice factors in the description of apparatus and in the text discussions of visuals, as the phenomenon occurs frequently in both these areas. On the other hand, while we have used material like that in example 8.8 with intermediate-level students, we find it best reserved for advanced students (usually postgraduates) who must read (and must possibly write) discourse of that nature.

The rhetorical–grammatical relationships illustrated and discussed in this chapter are taken up again in chapter 10, with suggestions for handling these topics in the classroom, including a sample individualized assignment relating to the grammatical problems we have found to be most troublesome to the non-native reader of EST discourse. Preceding this, in chapter 9 the two major lexical problems facing the non-native EST student are discussed and exemplified: the problems of sub-technical vocabulary and noun compounds.

9 Lexical problems in EST discourse

9.1 Introduction

The dictionary definition of the term 'lexis'[1] is 'all the words in a language' or 'all the words (in a language) that a person knows'. Our meaning is somewhat more restricted, referring only to the following three lexical areas: 1. technical vocabulary, 2. sub-technical vocabulary, and 3. noun compounds (sometimes called 'noun strings'). Technical vocabulary by itself does not pose enough of a problem for the majority of non-native students to need special attention in the classroom. (It seems rather pointless for a teacher not trained in science to 'teach' technical vocabulary to students who have already learned or are learning this highly specialized lexis in their subject-matter courses.)

Unfortunately, in the past many EST teachers unwittingly applied the same argument to sub-technical vocabulary and to noun compounds. As a result, the problems created by these two lexical areas were often overlooked. Too many early textbooks (before the mid-1970s) labelled themselves 'English for Science and Technology' because along with whatever grammatical approach was in vogue at the time, they included lists of presumably scientific or technical words under a heading such as 'Technical vocabulary'. Non-native students faced with a confusing sub-technical vocabulary or with unfamiliar noun strings naturally went to their bilingual and/or 'standard' English dictionaries, neither of which were designed to give them much help with these particular problems.

Once EST teachers and others in the field realized that even advanced students were having lexical problems that did not stem from their technical vocabularies nor from weaknesses in 'general English', there began some useful directed research. Our own work turned up three problem areas: 1. weaknesses in memorizing (which we were not prepared to cope with), 2. the – at that time – newly named field of sub-technical vocabulary, and 3. the less technical noun compounds. These last two problems are treated in some detail below.

9.2 Sub-technical vocabulary

As far as I have been able to determine this term was coined by Dr Ronayne Cowan of the University of Illinois (Urbana) some years ago. He defines sub-technical vocabulary as 'context-independent words which occur with high frequency across disciplines'.[2] This definition applies to those words that have the same meaning in several scientific or technical disciplines. To these words we have added 'those "common" words that occur with special meanings in specific scientific and technical fields'. Together, the two sets of words make up the English sub-technical vocabulary.

Another way of defining 'sub-technical' is to say that it refers to those words that have one or more 'general' English meanings and which in technical contexts take on extended meanings (technical, or specialized in some fashion).

While the more technical of these extended meanings are usually learned quickly (often in technical courses), the majority are seen in reading before they are heard or discussed either in the language or subject-matter classroom. Again, the result too often is that the students go to the dictionary and find no definitions that make sense in the context containing the word in question. (For some unexplained reason, few non-native science or technology students seem to have specialized dictionaries or, in many cases, even to be aware of their existence.) Whatever the reason, when students find that they have no definition to work with, they usually follow one of two procedures: those few with more confidence in both their language and subject-matter ability will try to create a meaningful definition from their own knowledge of the subject matter while the many less confident will ignore the particular piece of text and so lose the information the unidentified term and its surrounding context can give them.

A good example of problems with sub-technical vocabulary is one brought to us by a pre-medical student. He had found the phrase 'an arsenic-fast virus' in his medical reading. As the dictionaries he consulted were no help, he finally came to us. (Typically, he did not want to 'show his ignorance' to his subject-matter teacher by asking him.) He wanted to know if the word 'fast' in this context meant 'quick' or 'motionless' or even that a virus did not eat arsenic. The medical dictionary we consulted (and which he was not aware of) told us that in this usage 'fast' has the meaning of 'resistant to'. His phrase, therefore, had the meaning of 'a virus resistant to arsenic'.

We have always found 'fast' the most useful word to define in beginning a discussion of sub-technical vocabulary. Most students have been taught the several general meanings as well as the semi-technical use found most often on ships, 'to make something fast'. With this background available, it is usually quite easy to make students see very quickly that familiar words may have very unfamiliar meanings and, therefore, that a reputable dictionary in their subject-matter field (if one is available) would be a worthwhile (and long-term) investment.

Other words with extended meanings are given in chart 9.1 which has been designed as a handout to accompany a class discussion on sub-technical vocabulary.

CHART 9.1   SAMPLE SUB-TECHNICAL TERMS

1. *Base*
   Botany: 'The end of a plant member nearest the point of attachment to another member, usually of a different type.'
   Chemistry: 'A substance which tends to gain a proton.' 'A substance which reacts with acids to form salts.'
   Electronics: 'Part of a valve [US "tube"] where the pins that fit into holes in another electronic part are located.' 'The middle region of a transistor.'
   Navigation: 'In a navigation chain, the line which joins two of the stations.'

2. *Dog*
   Construction: 'A steel securing piece for fastening together two timbers.'
   Machining: 'A lathe carrier.'
   Mechanical engineering: 'An adjustable stop used in gears.'
   Petroleum engineering: 'A clutching attachment for withdrawing well-digging tools.'
   Railroading: 'A spike for securing rails to sleepers [US "ties"]'

3. *Fascia*
   Architecture: 'A board decorating a gutter around a building.'
   Automobile: 'The instrument panel.'
   Zoology: 'The connective tissue bands that join the fasciculi of a muscle.'

4. *Fast*
   Medicine: 'Resistant to.'
   Mining: 'A hard stratum under poorly consolidated ground.'
   Paint: 'Said of colours not affected by light, heat, damp.'

5. *Transport*
   Business: 'Any mechanical means of moving goods.'
   Literary: 'Enrapture' (archaic).
   Nuclear: 'The rate at which desired material is carried through a section of the processing cycle.'

9.3   Noun compounds

Noun compounds (also called noun strings) can be defined as two or more nouns plus necessary adjectives (and less often verbs and adverbs) that together make up a single concept; that is, the total expresses a 'single noun' idea. Noun compounding, while a characteristic of Germanic languages, is not one shared by all languages. It is a kind of shorthand: attempts to translate a complex compound into a language that does not compound usually result in long and unwieldy phrasing. That compounding is a natural process in so few languages makes it a special problem for the majority of non-native students.

Since compounding is frequently given time in intermediate and advanced ESL/EFL classes, the majority of students coming into a tertiary-level EST class can handle most two-word compounds, even those that may have a technical meaning. However, no matter how well students learn to analyze compounds into their component parts and, if necessary, translate them into their native languages, there are a great many compounds that refuse to yield to these procedures: while a travel book is most likely to be a book about travel, a telephone book is not a book about telephones. Copper wire and steel wire are wire made, respectively, of copper and steel. We cannot say the same about piano wire. When we look at the often complex compounds in scientific and technical discourse, we can see that the problem is magnified to the point where many are impossible of translation even by a native speaker unless that speaker knows the subject well.

Chart 9.2 summarizes the 'rules' for both understanding and producing compounds, whether technical or 'general'. While this summary has been found helpful to students, it can also be misleading as it suggests that most compounds can be understood by simply applying the 'rules'. But as we will see from chart 9.3 and the discussion following, the longer and more technical the compound, the less chance any but the most knowledgeable reader has of 'deciphering' it.

CHART 9.2   'RULES' FOR UNDERSTANDING AND PRODUCING
COMPOUNDS

> *'General English' examples*
> 1. A compound is a group of two or more nouns, plus such other parts of speech as are necessary, which expresses a 'single noun' idea. Compounds are usually formed from prepositional phrases or relative clauses and many can be back-formed into one or the other of these. However, many other compounds do not yield, either to back-formation or to translation into any 'logical' phrasing.
> 2. The simplest type of compounds are those formed from prepositional phrases with 'of': a desk drawer = a drawer of a desk; a table top = a top of a table.
> 3. In forming a compound from a phrase, the nouns in the phrase are put in reverse order: an advertisement (1) in a magazine (2) = a magazine (2) advertisement (1).
> 4. In a compound, if the noun (or nouns) that becomes the modifier is in the plural in the original phrase, it becomes singular in the

131

compound: a shelf for book*s* = a bookshelf (not a book*s*shelf as many non-native speakers would have it).

5. Prepositional phrases with 'for' also are often the basis for compounds. When these relate to activities either the compound or the base form – or both – usually contains a gerund: a device for open*ing* tins = a tin opener; a program for build*ing* roads = a road-building program.

6. Some compounds come from relative clauses: a book binder = a person (or machine) that binds books; a shoe store = a store in which shoes are sold.

7. Some compounds cannot be logically back-formed, nor can they always be simply translated: a department store = a store containing several different departments for selling different types of merchandise. Back-forming this would give us 'A store of departments', which is not a useful back-formation (nor a logical one), in that it fails to provide much information. The translation is obviously awkward and certainly not 'simple'. In the compound 'symphony music' we also have a problem with either back-formation or translation: if we try to back-form it, we get 'Music of/from a symphony', which is inaccurate; if we translate, we can get 'Music which is of the type called "symphonic"', but then we need to define 'symphonic'!

8. Compounds that lend themselves to translation can be translated in several ways. Some common ways are: a boat trip = a trip by/in a boat; laboratory equipment = equipment used in a laboratory; mathematics problem = a problem in mathematics (not *of* mathematics); physics laboratory = a laboratory where/in which experiments in physics are performed. (Even non-native students whose performance is well above average may need to be reminded that both 'mathematics' and 'physics' are singular nouns and so keep their 's' when acting as modifiers in compounds.)

Scientific and technical English examples
I. Compounds usually represent shorthand versions of the following:
   1. Prepositional phrases: a differential time domain equation = the time domain *of* a differential equation.
   2. Strings of prepositional phrases: momentum transfer experiments = experiments *of* the transfer *of* momentum.
   3. Nouns modified by relative clauses: automatic controller action = controller action which is automatic.
   4. Nouns modified by gerund phrases: a fluid bed reactor = a reactor containing a fluid bed.
   5. Combinations of the above: an air pressure device = a device *which* signals the pressure *of* air; a quiescent state fluid bed reactor = a reactor contain*ing* a fluid bed *which/that* is in a state of quiescence.

II.   Notes:
1.   The most commonly used prepositions in scientific and technical compounds are *of*, *for*, *in*, *on*, and *with*.
2.   In addition to the relatives in their base forms (who, which, that) translations (or back-formations) of compounds use relatives as prepositional objects: *in which, for which, on which*, etc.
3.   In some cases EST compound elements are joined by conjunctions when translated; this conjunction is usually 'and': a self-contained automatic controller device = a device which controls (something) *and* which is automatic *and* self-contained.

In chart 9.3 the compounds are divided into four categories based on their length and the complexity of paraphrasing them or of returning them to their original form.

CHART 9.3   COMPOUNDS CATEGORIZED BY LENGTH AND
DIFFICULTY OF PARAPHRASING

I.   *Simple*
1.   Metal shaft = a shaft made of metal.
2.   Metal spring = a spring made of metal.
3.   Metal cutter = *not* a cutter made of metal but an instrument used to cut metal.

II.   *Complex*
1.   Liquid storage vessel = a vessel for storage of liquids/for storing liquids (*not* as some non-native students would have it, a liquid vessel used for storage!).
2.   Transport sector investment = investment in that sector of the economy which concerns transport – the movement of goods and people.
3.   Automated nozzle brick grinder = a grinder of nozzle bricks (a type of brick) (*not* a grinder of bricks, the grinder having a nozzle which is automated).

III.   *More complex* (See below for a discussion of these examples.)
1.   Aisle seat speech interference level.
2.   Long-term surveillance test planning.
3.   Swine salted viscera.

IV.   *Very complex* (See below for a discussion of these examples.)
1.   Full swivel steerable non-retracting tail wheel overhaul.
2.   Heterogeneous graphite moderated natural uranium fueled nuclear reactor.
3.   Split damper inertially coupled passive gravity gradient satellite attitude control system.

[The above 'more complex' and 'very complex' compounds present difficulties even to native speakers. Even 'complex' compounds can

133

create problems for the reader without a knowledge of the field. 'Automated nozzle brick grinder' is a good example of this: most readers' initial response (including our own) is to assume that 'nozzle' is part of the grinding machinery, not a type of brick.

The three examples under 'more complex' compounds all require explanation, sometimes even to experts in fields other than those represented by the compounds. 'Aisle-seat speech-interference level' is taken from an airplane manufacturing company report and refers to acoustic tests made to determine the level of interference with speech between an attendant and a passenger who is sitting in an aisle seat (on a medium sized jet airplane). As is so often the case with compounds of this type, the problem here is one of ambiguity. On first reading one wonders if there is 'interference *with* speech taking place at an aisle seat' or 'interference *from* speech issuing from an aisle seat'. 'Long term surveillance test planning' refers to plans for educational tests, these to be subject to surveillance over a long period of time. 'Swine salted viscera' are not, as the order of the elements suggests, 'viscera salted with swine' but the viscera of swine, the swine themselves having been salted.

Each of the 'very complex' compounds illustrates a different construction and the discussion here presents different ways of solving the paraphrase problem. Each compound requires a thorough knowledge of the subject matter to be understood and even then numbers 2 and 3 had to be 'translated' by their writers before their colleagues could understand. 'Full swivel steerable non-retracting tail wheel overhaul' is from an airplane maintenance manual. All of the modifiers of 'overhaul' form a unit with the headword of this compound within a compound being 'tail wheel'; thus we have the overhaul of an airplane tail wheel (or of a wheel which retracts into the tail of the airplane), this tail wheel having the characteristics of being non-retractable, steerable, and capable of making a complete swivel. The involved appearing compound 'A heterogeneous graphite moderated natural uranium fueled nuclear reactor' becomes somewhat easier to read if a few punctuation symbols are used to clarify the problem of which word modifies which other word (or words): 'A heterogeneous, graphite-moderated, natural-uranium-fueled nuclear reactor'. The last example, 'A split damper inertially coupled passive gravity gradient satellite attitude control system' may hold the record for length, containing as it does eleven elements plus the indefinite article. This can also be improved by punctuation: 'A split damper, inertially coupled, passive-gravity-gradient, satellite attitude control system'. However, this amount of clarification was still not enough for the writer's colleagues, one of whom finally suggested the following translation: 'A system for controlling the attitude (degree of angle from the perpendicular) of a satellite, this system operating with the following characteristics: it has a split damper and is coupled (joined) by inertia and has its gradient determined by allowing gravity to take control (with no

effort to overcome gravity).' While the aerospace engineers who
accepted this translation may have felt comfortable with it, I find the
translation only a little less puzzling than the original. It is, of course,
the type of compound that technical writers should be discouraged to
write, whatever the provocation.]

While such compounds as these last examples are seldom written by
anyone but the professional scientist or engineer, we find quite daunting
examples in material designed for technicians and technical trainees. For
example, this compound comes from a manual for training welders:
'Conventional resistance lap seam welding method'! An almost classic
example of this type of writing is example 9.1, an excerpt from a
troubleshooting manual written for airline technicians, many of whom
are non-native speakers. The compounds are shown in italics.

EXAMPLE 9.1   NOUN COMPOUNDS IN A TECHNICAL MANUAL

If the EGT [*Exhaust gas temperature*] reaches the *trip point* of the
overload temperature switch (704 to 718°) the *sensing circuit* in the
overtemperature control switch will de-energize the *thermostat
selector solenoid valve* and the *bleed air solenoid*. This causes the
load control valve to close (removes the load) and switches the
thermostat to the *acceleration mode*. When the EGT drops to a
nominal 205° below the *switch trip point*, the *overtemperature
control switch* will reset, energizing the *thermostat selector
solenoid valve* and the *bleed air solenoid*. This will cause the *load
control valve* to open and switch the thermostat to the *load control
mode*.

[Source: *737 APU Troubleshooting Guide*, p. 51.]

[This brief paragraph contains fifteen compounds, three of which are
two-word compounds, ten are three-word compounds, and two are
four-word compounds. Three of the three-word compounds are used
twice as is the four-word compound. If we eliminate the duplicates
we still have eleven separate, mostly complex compounds in a
paragraph of 102 words.]

9.4   Application

For purposes of classroom discussion it is convenient to divide compounds into the four categories illustrated above. However, we find that
spending much time on the more complex and very complex compounds
is a futile pursuit, as it is difficult, if not impossible, for someone not
versed in the subject to translate most of them. Whether students are
native or non-native speakers seems to make little difference in this

respect; learning the 'rules' of translating compounds does not make understanding the technical ones easier. Finally, those difficult compounds that are relevant to the students' work will, as in the case of technical terms, be explained to them in the appropriate subject-matter classes. In our experience it is more useful to the student to work with simple and perhaps complex compounds and to give assignments that relate these to improving both reading and writing skills. Using the individualized assignment approach – first discussed in chapter 4 – we ask the students to bring from their subject-matter reading samples of various types of compounds. Many of these can be used as bases for class discussions with stress on translating and paraphrasing.

For those compounds too technical or too difficult to use in the classroom, we have devised two approaches. The first is to have the student ask his or her teachers to explain them. As many non-native students are hesitant to show their ignorance before subject-matter teachers (but not before English teachers!), our second procedure is to make lists of the more complex and very complex compounds brought to us and go ourselves to the appropriate teachers for the necessary information. This method has the advantage of creating a file that can be used with future classes. (Unfortunately, none of the above advice copes with the problem of our students becoming professional scientists and engineers and being faced with impossible compounds in their professional reading.)

The procedure described above for having students bring difficult compounds to their English class also works with troublesome sub-technical terms. With either compounds or sub-technical terms the individualization process works well as a springboard for writing exercises. The most successful procedure that we have found is to collect lists of compounds and sub-technical terms from the students (in separate assignments) and to hold these for several days. During this interval several of the terms that seem most useful can be marked – circled or underlined, for example. The lists are then returned to students with instructions to choose, let us say, two of the marked terms and use each in a paragraph whose context helps explain their meanings. Depending on the time available to the teacher and the nature of the class, this type of exercise can be done in class or given as an outside assignment. It can also be tied in later with review work; for example, have the students write paragraphs that use certain rhetorical techniques and/or rhetorical functions and, at the same time, use some of the compounds or sub-technical terms marked by the teacher. A composite individualized assignment for lexical work is given in chapter 10.

10   Teaching the rhetorical process

10.1   Introduction

This final chapter has two functions: the first is a kind of mini-course that takes the reader through a complete presentation of the rhetorical process as given in an academic classroom, the second examines the more difficult problems that in our experience are most likely to appear in teaching EST students and suggests classroom oriented solutions. The two functions are not treated separately; rather, the problems are taken up at that point in the 'mini-course' where they would occur naturally in a classroom situation.

Taking our course will be a class made up as follows: twenty students, ranging from undergraduates (the majority) to a small number working for advanced degrees in one of the sciences or in engineering. The fields of study represented include all of engineering, the physical and natural sciences, pre-medicine and dentistry, nursing, nutrition, and home economics. Eight of the students are women, six of them evenly divided between nursing, nutrition, and home economics and the remaining two in pre-medicine. Of the twelve men, one is in pre-dentistry, two are in nutrition (also known as food chemistry), and the remainder in engineering and the sciences. Their abilities in English are as varying as their ages and interests, although all are considered capable of handling the language at upper-intermediate level and capable of handling the rhetorical concepts as well.

As I pointed out in section 2.2, chapter 2, we need not think only in terms of academic students and academically oriented classrooms while reading through the chapters detailing the steps in the rhetorical process. This is equally true of the presentation of the mini-course in this chapter. Although I use a hypothetical academically oriented EST class as the basis for the presentation, this does not mean that the course could not be modified to fit the circumstances of another type of EST class. For example, we can tailor the process to fit, let us say, a more vocationally oriented class by shifting emphasis from definition and classification to instructions and visual–verbal relationships but leaving description much the same.

10.2   Course pattern

Over the years we have experimented with several ways of presenting the rhetorical process, with the pattern given below being the most successful. The time shown for each part of the process is an average based on several years of teaching the course and is not intended to represent an ideal figure but only to provide guidelines.

Suggested course pattern

I. *Introductory*
    The overall procedure for the course is explained. Types of reading and writing assignments are discussed briefly. A loose-leaf file is shown and its use and value explained (see 8 below). Several technical and general dictionaries are named and discussed (and, if possible, shown).
    Time. One class hour. (Class hours vary from 45 to 55 minutes. Ours are 50 minutes.)

II. *The rhetorical process*
    1. The rhetorical point to be studied (paragraph, rhetorical technique, rhetorical function, or grammatical or lexical element) is presented and briefly explained. Examples labeled with the relevant rhetorical feature(s) are handed out and discussed in detail, with the given rhetorical point stressed. Once the students participate in the discussions, these become what we call workshops. (In the first discussion/workshop there will, of course, be only the one rhetorical point. However, as the rhetorical process is cumulative, each point already discussed will be seen to relate to the subsequent points. As a result, the time required for each rhetorical feature may increase.)
       Time. For the paragraph, one hour for each of the two elements (correspondences and cores) is adequate. For the rhetorical techniques (during which some of the information on the paragraph must be presented again), two hours on the natural orders and one hour on the logical orders is usually sufficient. The rhetorical functions require more time as each is best treated separately. Also it is necessary to bring into the discussion the previously taught rhetorical features (for example, physical description cannot be thoroughly understood without an understanding of its relation to space order). The time required for description and visual–verbal relationships is normally one class period for each; definition and classification can take three hours together; and instructions need one class hour for the average academic group.
       (If the grammatical features relating to the rhetorical functions

138

are taught at this time, then more time per function is needed. See 6 below.)

2. In workshops, unlabeled examples are handed out and analyzed orally for the relevant rhetorical feature(s). After sufficient discussion, if the 'correct' analysis to the examples has not come from the students, this is either written on the blackboard, shown on an overhead projector, or dictated. The students are expected to note the answers on their unlabeled handouts, these to be stored in their loose-leaf files.

   Time. While all workshops but the first should include the rhetorical points made in previous workshops, the amount of time spent on each need not necessarily increase by much the total time spent on any of the steps in the rhetorical process as the workshop times are included into the times given above. However, if more time is required (for example, to make certain that a difficult point has been understood), we suggest two hours held 'in reserve'. Should these extra hours not be needed for workshops, we can use them for brief tests or save them for problem periods later. (See 5 below.)

3. If the rhetorical feature has not been grasped by the majority of the class, part or all of the above procedure can be repeated with other examples.

   Time. At the most, one half hour is devoted to each of the rhetorical points not clearly understood. We find that setting aside one hour of extra time is usually more than sufficient.

4. The next step is to make individualized assignments based on the reading the students are doing for their technical courses. Some of the examples submitted to fulfil the assignments will be found useful either as models, bases for discussion, or selections to be used in revision for examinations. With permission of the students who handed them in, copies of these can be kept and used either with the current class or with future classes. It is useful to put some of the 'best' examples (both the best 'good' and the best 'bad' examples) on transparencies, with, of course, identification removed.

   Time. We find that short, fairly frequent assignments produce better results than do long ones given less often, as receiving assignments more frequently allows the teacher to follow the students' progress more closely. (Longer assignments can be given periodically as a kind of 'test'.) We usually expect an assignment to be turned in either two class periods after it has been made (for example, an assignment made on a Monday would be turned in Friday) or if made on a Friday, it could easily be handed in the following Monday.

5. The results of the individualized assignments make clear whether a) more workshops are needed; b) brief tests should be given; or c) the next step in the process should be begun.

   Time. How much time should be given to additional workshops is a function of how much time is available. If more time than already set aside is taken, we may have to curtail our writing program.

6. During presentation of some of the rhetorical features, grammatical and lexical problems can appear quite naturally. When this happens, our procedure is to set aside temporarily the discussion on the rhetorical feature and work instead on the grammatical or lexical element and its relationship to the rhetorical feature. Once this relationship is understood, the discussion is shifted back to the rhetoric. If this procedure is followed, later work on the grammatical points seldom needs to be more than a brief mention.

   Time. I suggest the following average additional time for discussing each grammatical point with its relevant rhetorical function:

   Description: a) passive–stative distinctions, one class hour; b) specialized uses of the definite article, one class hour; c) non-temporal choice of tense, half class hour.

   Definition and classification: relative clauses, half class hour together.

   Instructions: a) inconsistent use of the definite article, one class hour; b) non-standard meanings of the modals 'should', 'can', and 'may', half class hour.

   Visual–verbal relationships: non-temporal choice of tense in text accompanying a visual, half class hour.

7. If writing is to be emphasized in later stages of the course, assignments for any lengthy work should be given far enough in advance for the procedure in section 10.9 to be followed. The basic factor in this procedure is the amount of in-class supervision teachers either feel that they can give or wish to give to student writing. This supervision can vary from almost zero (merely giving and receiving assignments) to complete control by having all the writing done in the class.

8. One of the features of the course that students feel is most helpful is the requirement that they keep their examples and analyses of the various rhetorical, grammatical, and lexical features in order in a loose-leaf file and that this be handed in with each new assignment. The advantage to the students is that they then have an organized record of the work they have done along with evaluations of each assignment. The advantage to the teachers is that

they can determine improvement of each student at any stage during the course.

10.3   The rhetorical approach: preliminary remarks

After trying several orders of presentation of the rhetorical material, we found the one given below the most successful. Our course to teach non-native students to read (and secondarily to write) EST discourse was originally developed to fit into a ten-week term, the class meeting three days per week, with each meeting lasting a 'class' hour (that is, 50 minutes) for a total of 30 contact hours per term. Teachers who have used the rhetorical process in courses divided differently have told us that they had little difficulty in tailoring the material by spending extra time on the more difficult points. This works especially with upper-elementary or lower-intermediate groups where it is often possible to leave out those points that may be too advanced for their levels of reading and instead concentrating on those more useful to the students (for example, a class of vocational trainees needs more time on the rhetoric of instructions and visual–verbal relationships than on, let us say, the more esoteric forms of definition.)

The following discussion treats the rhetorical features in the same order as they are treated in the preceding chapters. I have not shown any of the various brief tests we injected at intervals as this part of any course is always governed by time and by the individual teacher's way of working. However, in section 10.9 I have added suggestions on how to exercise maximum control over a major writing project designed as a test of the students' abilities to find and use the rhetorical features stressed during the course.

Introductory presentation

We make the following points in a handout to the students in the early sessions:
1. The class will be conducted through explanations and discussions of the rhetorical process and through workshops designed to give practice in applying the process.
2. The course covers five major areas of scientific and technical English. For each of these areas the procedure is as follows:
   a) We begin with an introductory explanation of the rhetorical point(s) to be studied and of the assignments that will grow out of the discussion.
   b) Following the introductory explanations, you will receive handouts that have examples of the rhetorical features of the point

141

being studied. These handouts are labeled so that each main rhetorical feature is identified. This material should be put in a loose-leaf file and kept for reference. You are expected to bring this file to each class meeting.

c) A second set of handouts will be given out once the discussion of the first set is finished. This second set will be unlabeled and will be used as the basis for further discussion in workshops. From the previous discussions and from your labeled handouts, you should be able to find the main rhetorical features on the unlabeled handouts. Once the concepts are clear in your mind you should transfer the information to the margins of your unlabeled examples and put these in your loose-leaf reference file.

d) Assignments: you will be asked to go to the books you read for your subject-matter courses (both textbooks and supplementary reading) and find examples of the rhetorical point just discussed. If possible, these are to be photocopied (if not, copied carefully by hand) and the copy trimmed and pasted on the size of paper that fits your file. Instructions for labeling and writing an analysis of your material will be given out with the assignment.

e) Your final assignment will be a research paper that contains examples of all of the rhetorical elements discussed during the course. Details will be given out later.

(*To the teacher*: The 'Rhetorical process chart', p. 11 above, should be handed out as soon as it can be used as a basis for discussion. If it is referred to frequently during the introductory sessions, the students should (might) get in the habit of bringing it to class to be used as a reference tool in conjunction with the material in their loose-leaf files.)

Comments on the rhetorical points and on assignments made for each major step in the rhetorical process along with suggested solutions to problems that arise in the EST classroom are given in sections 10.4 through 10.8. Section 10.9 discusses procedure for exercising various amounts of control over writing assignments. It also suggests a way of completely controlling a lengthy end-of-term writing assignment designed to test the students' grasp of the course content.

10.4 Teaching the paragraph

A sample individualized assignment on the paragraph is given in chart 4.1, p. 42 above. In this assignment the students are asked to go to their subject-matter reading and find six different types of paragraphs. As noted earlier, this is a composite assignment and is clearly too long, especially for a first attempt at a type of exercise that few if any of the students have done before. An adequate beginning assignment might be to require any two of the first four types of paragraph, while for a class that shows a strong grasp of the concepts, an assignment can be made from either the first four or the last two types.

The instructions for assignments such as these – and for any others in which the students are asked to bring samples of printed material – should stress that each example is to be accompanied by a complete source reference: we find it useful to give the students a handout containing standard bibliographic forms to use as guides. (Unfortunately, we realized a bit late the need to insist on full references; as a result many of our 'best' examples brought by students are quoted without sources.)

Because few, if any, students will have dealt with this type of assignment before, detailed comments on the first assignment in each rhetorical area can be helpful, especially if they indicate the place and type of error and suggest corrections.

The following checklist, developed by trial and error over the years, offers guidelines for evaluating these early assignments:

1. Have all of the requirements of the assignment been fulfilled? (For example, is the correspondence exemplified the one wanted?) Are the paragraphs correctly labeled as to type? Are the core statements underlined, if this has been requested?)
2. Have all the rhetorical, grammatical, and lexical elements called for been marked (circled or otherwise indicated)?
3. Have 'non-native' errors been copied into the sample texts?
4. Are the sources of the sample texts as complete as possible?

To test the students' knowledge of the basic ideas of the paragraph a minimum of two assignments is usually necessary: one to check for an understanding of the concept of cores; the other to check for an understanding of the concept of correspondences. Either or both of these can be tested by handing out unlabeled sample paragraphs and having the students label and analyze them in the classroom. Since it is impossible to cover separately all the fields of study represented in the average class in this way, we resort to the type of exercises discussed in chapter 4, section 4.4 on 'Parallelism'. Sometimes it is necessary to continue with this 'general' approach until the students show that they understand the principles of the paragraph sufficiently to be able to move on to the next step in the rhetorical process.

However, while this type of approach is necessary to provide the students with a sound grasp of the basics of the paragraph, real understanding seems to come only when they actually discover paragraphs functioning in discourse related to their own subject-matter areas. The one way that we have found to ensure the students making such 'discoveries' is to individualize their major assignments, as outlined in chapter 4, section 4.6. Also, as noted earlier, this approach has the advantage of giving some feel of 'genuineness' to the normally artificial atmosphere of the English language classroom.

10.5   Teaching the rhetorical techniques

The discussions on the rhetorical techniques are found in chapter 3, sub-section 3.2.2, and in chapter 6. Chart 6.1, pp. 53–4 above, lists the most common rhetorical techniques (also called 'patterns of paragraph development') that are found in EST discourse and shows the 'key' terms signalling that a particular rhetorical technique is being used – or is going to be used – by the writer. This list is useful as a basis for initial discussion on the rhetorical techniques as well as a reference for the students.

The more 'advanced' the discourse (that is, the closer to 'peer writing'), the more we find writers leaving out the 'key' terms. The rhetorical technique being used is then normally indicated by context and/or juxtaposition of statements. Thus we have covertly signalled or 'implied' rather than overtly stated rhetorical techniques. While these seldom cause problems for the native reader, the same is not true of most non-native readers, since very few 'feel' what are often quite subtle relationships. The solution to this problem that we have found most successful is to have the students learn virtually by rote the key terms along with the rhetorical techniques that they indicate and then have them practice recognizing the more covert signals of context and juxtaposition.

For readers to be able to recognize quickly and accurately that the writer is going to express a specific relationship between two pieces of information is a skill invaluable in improving their reading speed and comprehension. For this reason, we spend as much class time as is necessary to make certain that determining these relationships has become an (at least partially) automatic process. Our procedure is, again, to follow the pattern of the other individualized assignments and have the students find examples in their own subject-matter reading of 'implied' rhetorical techniques and in their analyses to state precisely what the relationships are and what covert signals gave them this information.

By adding this type of individualized assignment to those given in chapter 6, we can create assignments much more complex and demanding than those given for the paragraph alone (chapter 5). We can, for example, ask for paragraphs that not only illustrate a given rhetorical technique but have a one-to-one (or one-to-more-than-one) correspondence and, as well, indicate the rhetorical relationships by a 'key' term or by juxtaposition and/or context. We can also ask for paragraphs that combine two or more techniques: for example, process time order and causality or specific space order and contrast.

Depending on the nature of a given class, preparing the students for assignments of the type described above often requires several hours of discussion and workshop practice. The examples given in chapter 6 are useful both in class discussion and in workshops since they are carefully chosen illustrations of the rhetorical techniques as these are found most commonly in written EST discourse. We have had our best success in giving these out as unlabeled examples after handing out and discussing simpler labeled examples of each technique. Our procedure for a 'typical' class is as follows:

1. A general discussion of the concept 'rhetorical technique', including the categorization of the techniques into 'natural orders' and 'logical orders' (or, if preferred into 'orders' and/or 'patterns') and of the way writers have of showing the relationship of an item of information to another.
2. The presentation of labeled examples of 'time order' and as much discussion as is necessary *before proceeding to the next technique.* (That is, the discussion and initial exemplification of time order should be finished before space order is begun.)
3. A workshop in which the students make written analyses of unlabeled examples of the technique being studied. If these analyses are discussed orally we often get a bonus of oral practice when the students disagree over one another's analyses.
4. At this point, either of two procedures can be followed: individualized assignments on the technique just covered can be handed out or these can be postponed until each technique has been presented.
5. Whichever procedure is followed, once each technique has been discussed and illustrated (and, if desired at this point, tested by assignments), the problems of a) 'implied' relationships and b) combinations of relationships are worked on.
6. If the individualized assignments have not yet been given, they should be handed out at this point. However, as a rule we find it more satisfactory to give out short individualized assignments after each technique has been covered and then to give out a 'broader' assignment as a kind of overall revision.

An example of an individualized assignment that could be made at the end of the last workshop on the 'natural' orders is given in chart 10.1.

CHART 10.1   SAMPLE INDIVIDUALIZED ASSIGNMENT: RHETORICAL
TECHNIQUES

    I. From your own subject-matter reading bring examples of the following types of paragraph development:
        1. time chronology;
        2. time process;
        3. space order;
        4. causality and result
           a) mixed with time process;
           b) containing no time element.

    II. Also bring examples of the following:

1. a time order paragraph (chronology or process time) illustrating a one-to-more-than-one correspondence;
2. a time or space order paragraph with an implied (not stated) core.

At the top of each example, state the main type of development (for example, 'Time process'). Within each paragraph, underline the core statement and circle any key terms that mark your main type of development (that is, 'time' words or 'space' words, etc.). If the core is not stated, then beneath the paragraph, write out what you think would be a good core statement. Beneath the paragraph *give its source.* In a separate paragraph below your example, make as complete a rhetorical analysis as you can, using the sample analyses given in your handouts as guides.

[While this is clearly too long to be given out as a single assignment, it does suggest the scope possible in individualizing exercises. An assignment given out after the logical patterns have been presented could well include the above with additions such as asking for time or space order paragraphs using comparison or contrast or exemplification, etc. as their secondary patterns of development. In the instructions given out with assignments such as these, students can also be asked to indicate the secondary as well as the primary way(s) in which their example paragraphs are developed.]

Once all of the rhetorical techniques are presented and tested, it is fruitful to review them in the context of the paragraph; that is, stressing the cores and correspondences in the paragraphs that contain examples of the rhetorical techniques. As noted above, this allows for a final set of individualized assignments that can incorporate both rhetorical features studied to date.

10.6   Teaching the rhetorical functions

The discussions on the rhetorical functions are found in chapter 3, subsection 3.2.3, and chapter 7. Although there is no single summary chart for the rhetorical functions as there is for the rhetorical techniques, each function has its own chart listing the kinds and amounts of information the reader should expect to get from that particular function or subfunction. If possible, these charts should be handed out at the beginning of the presentation of each function to make them available both for class discussion and as references to help the students in their assignments and during tests and workshops.

As noted earlier in this book, the rhetorical functions are the core of the rhetorical approach. Looking back at the 'Rhetorical process chart', p. 11

above, we can see that the rhetorical functions given for Level C are in the best position to provide basic information: by their very nature the rhetorical functions give the reader the types of information most frequently found in written EST discourse. Also this information is usually carried by the conceptual paragraph, thus providing the reader with a functional and flexible organizational unit.

If the concepts of paragraph and rhetorical techniques are already understood, students usually find the rhetorical functions easy to relate to the rhetorical process. However, because of their importance to the total discourse and because of the sometimes difficult grammatical relationships often best taught concurrently with them, we prefer to 'over-present' the rhetorical functions and end this phase of the course with a thorough revision of the entire rhetorical process given to this point.

Our most successful pattern of presentation is the following:
1. An initial presentation explains what the term 'rhetorical functions' encompasses, with very brief samples of each of the functions presented in context; each function is then given detailed treatment before the next is presented; the order of presentation is the same as that in chapter 7 – description, definition, classification, instructions, and visual–verbal relationships (but see step 5 below.)
2. Labeled examples are handed out and discussed in detail.
3. Unlabeled examples are handed out and used first in class discussion and then in a workshop; this latter is followed by a short individualized assignment and/or a brief test.
4. Based on the results of the assignment (or test), either review is made as necessary or the discussion passes on to the next rhetorical function.
5. At the end of the presentation of the first three functions – description, definition, and classification – a larger individualized assignment is made: this assignment asks the students to find examples of each of the three functions and also to find examples of paragraphs in which two or more of the functions work together.
6. The same type of assignment is made after the two remaining functions – instructions and visual–verbal relationships – have been presented.
7. Depending again on the nature of the class being taught, if necessary a final assignment can follow further review (also if necessary). A useful assignment at this point is to have the students try to find in their reading examples of discourse that include several of the functions. A variation on this type of assignment is one that asks for combinations of the three steps in the rhetorical process discussed to date; for example, definition paragraphs that also include, let us say, physical description and have a one-to-more-than-one correspondence, or any similar combinations.

Sample individualized assignments for each of the rhetorical functions are given in the following discussions, in which each function is treated in a separate sub-section in some detail in order to stress the points that we have found to be most important for that particular function.

10.6.1 Description

The discussions pertaining to the three types of description are in chapter 3, sub-section 3.2.3, and chapter 7, section 7.2. Chart 7.1, p. 73, is the basis for an introductory class presentation. Following this, each type of description is taken up separately: unlabeled and then labeled examples are handed out and, if needed, a short workshop is held before moving on to the next type of description.

We find that the discussions are best handled by putting stress on the kinds of information each type of description should provide the reader. For example, if the 'Canal bottom sampler' (example 7.1, p. 72) is used, questions can be asked such as 'What physical points does the writer consider important – dimension? colour? texture? materials?' 'Does the writer describe the purpose of the device? That is, does he give the function of the whole, or just the functions of some of the parts?' 'Why did he choose such and such a part – instead of some others – to describe functionally?' 'How many steps are there in the process description given in this text?'

Once all three types of description have been covered and the students seem to understand the rhetorical concepts involved, then individualized assignments can be given. At this stage, these can be simple – limiting themselves to having the students find paragraphs illustrating the different types of description (or combinations of these) – or they can be complex, taking advantage of the work already done with paragraphs and the rhetorical techniques. Writing assignments, if given, can follow the same patterns. A sample individualized assignment is shown in chart 10.2.

CHART 10.2   SAMPLE INDIVIDUALIZED ASSIGNMENT: DESCRIPTION

> From your subject-matter reading, find examples of the following types of paragraphs:
>
> 1. Find paragraphs that are mostly (or completely)
>   a) physical description;
>   b) function description;
>   c) process description.
> The paragraph of physical description must show clearly the use of space order; the paragraph of function description, the use of causality and result; and the paragraph of process description, the use

of process time and of causality and result. This paragraph should not be in the form of a set of instructions.

2. Find two paragraphs that mix types of description in different proportions –
   a) a mixture of physical and function description;
   b) a mixture of physical and process description (plus some function description if it occurs in your example).
There are no restrictions on which rhetorical techniques are used in these paragraphs.

Once the individualized assignments have been done satisfactorily, there is a choice of procedure: the grammatical areas that relate to the rhetoric of description (for example, the passive–stative distinction) can be brought up for discussion, or the class can continue working with the rhetorical functions and can give the grammatical–rhetorical relationships separately later. We find the former the more satisfactory procedure: to wait until all of the rhetorical functions are presented before picking up the related grammatical elements at a later date usually requires revision of some of the rhetorical points in order for the students to see the relationship between a specific point of grammar and a given rhetorical function. Presenting the related grammatical point (and at times bringing in pertinent lexis) immediately following work on a given rhetorical function allows the relationships to be seen more easily and more quickly.

Chapter 8 is the source for the information on the grammatical elements that relate to the rhetorical functions. Specifically, the rhetoric of description is concerned with passive–stative distinctions in the three types of description (section 8.2), with the specialized use of the definite article in physical description (section 8.4), and with the non-temporal use of tense in the physical description of apparatus (sub-section 5.1). In our experience these grammatical elements are best treated at the end of the classroom work on description and in the order given above.

An alternative procedure is to divide the discussion of the rhetorical–grammatical relationships into two parts: the treatment of the rhetorical function is followed by a few examples and a short discussion of the grammatical element (or elements) related to that function. The subject can then be treated more completely after the full presentation of the rhetorical functions has ended and that on the rhetorical–grammatical relationships has been taken up. This approach has the advantage of allowing the teacher to judge during the initial presentation how well the students have understood the several sets of relationships discussed and, therefore, how much time they will need to spend on each relationship when the rhetorical–grammatical discussions are held.

10.6.2 Definition

The discussions on definition are in chapter 3, sub-section 3.2.3, and chapter 7, section 7.3. The summary of information provided by each type of definition is in chart 7.3, p. 79. This chart is useful both as a basis for a preliminary discussion of definition and as a reference for the students.

We find that definition is best presented in the order given in chapter 7, section 7.3, with each type treated separately for purposes of class discussion and early workshop practice. Once each of the three types of 'simple' definition is seen to be understood (again through the use of labeled handouts, unlabeled handouts, and short workshops), it is usually quite easy to move into the more difficult area of complex definition.

As most examples of simple definition are in single sentences, it might seem that we are dealing here with an area that does not make use of discourse contexts. However, these single-definition sentences are seldom found in isolation; those that the students bring from their subject-matter reading are almost invariably the core statements of paragraphs that function as one or another type of expanded definition. Although it is necessary for the students to see this relationship between definition and discourse units fairly early in their study of the rhetoric of definition, we find that while teaching the basic concepts of definition, we are more likely to have quicker positive results if we keep our examples at the single sentence level – but only during this initial period.

In our experience spending too much time on simple definitions as exemplified in single sentences can be self defeating. Once the students have clearly grasped 1) the amounts and kinds of information each type of simple definition should provide the reader and 2) the essential structural differences between the three types, then it is more useful to move on to definitions in their discourse contexts. Each type of simple definition is, of course, treated as part of a larger discourse unit in the work on complex definition, both when the students make analyses of their subject-matter reading and when they transfer to production by writing their own definitions. It is worth noting here that having the students write definitions is a much more useful exercise when these are required to be in some kind of context. Students benefit very little in terms of practicing organization, of achieving syntactic and semantic correctness, etc. by producing mostly single-sentence definitions. (We should also point out that only the most advanced students usually benefit from being asked to practice writing implicit definitions.)

Chart 10.3 illustrates a brief individualized assignment designed to follow the discussions on both simple and complex definition.

CHART 10.3   SAMPLE INDIVIDUALIZED ASSIGNMENT: DEFINITION

From your subject-matter reading, find examples of the following types of paragraphs:
1. Find a paragraph that has a formal definition as its core generalization. This paragraph must be expanded by description or example or operation.
2. Find a second paragraph that has a formal definition as its core generalization. This paragraph must be expanded by explication.
3. Find a paragraph that has as its core a semi-formal definition. This paragraph must be expanded by function description or example.
4. Find a paragraph that has a non-formal definition as its core statement. This paragraph can be expanded by any of the means discussed in class.

[Note: If experience means anything, the teacher will find that assignments 2 and 4 are the most difficult for the students to fulfil: assignment 2 because a) explication is not always easy to find and b) because the students do not always recognize explication when they see it; and assignment 4 because not many EST sentences have non-formal definitions as their cores. When it proved too difficult for some of the students to find examples of sentences with non-formal definitions as cores (the discourse in some fields contains very few examples of non-formal definitions), we would have the students substitute either a second paragraph having a semi-formal definition as the core or a paragraph containing a non-formal definition and another statement as the core.]

The grammatical element that relates to the rhetoric of definition is not treated in the same way as are the passive–stative distinctions and the specialized use of the definite article with the rhetoric of description since here we are concerned only with relative clauses and their substitute structure. As the relative or its equivalent is found in all formal definitions, the students need to work with these early in the discussions on definition. However, as most EST students are assumed to be adequate in the basics of English when they enter the course, it is usually necessary to plan only for a brief review of the relative and its substitute as found in formal definitions (the '-ing' form, usually of 'to have', as in 'An arachnid is an invertebrate animal *having* [as a substitute for *which/that has*] eight legs ...'). Occasionally, we find other verbs used in present participial form (such as 'possessing', 'displaying', 'showing', etc.) and these should be noted.

If the students are expected to produce formal definitions then more work on the relatives might be necessary, especially with those students whose languages demand an inserted pronoun after the relative (for example, 'An arachnid is an invertebrate animal which *it* has eight legs

...'). If this extra work on relatives is needed, useful exercises at the single-sentence level can be found in many EST texts.

Lexical problems, particularly those discussed in chapter 9, can arise for non-native students when they work with the kinds of definitions common in scientific and technical discourse: they frequently find 'general' words used with specific technical meanings or, more often, they run against puzzling (perhaps unsolvable) noun compounds. Exercises on these lexical problems are given in section 10.8. These exercises are individualized to perform a multiple function. First, they make learners aware of the best ways to get meaning out of terms they may have previously skipped over in their reading. Second, they give practice in recognizing and creating definitions. Third, the definitions the students create can be used as bases for practice in writing expanded definition paragraphs.

10.6.3 Classification

Classification (discussed in chapter 3, sub-section 3.2.3 and chapter 7, section 7.4) is best taught (like description and definition) by first treating each of the three types – complete, partial, and implicit classification – with the majority of time spent on making clear the basic concepts as they are found in complete classification (see chart 7.4, p. 93). Unless the students grasp the concepts involved in complete classification they will have difficulty understanding partial classification and little if any chance of being able to abstract implicit classifying information from a text. (Despite classification being an everyday activity on the part of most humans and especially for those involved in academic work, it is surprising how much difficulty many seem to have in understanding the concept or even in recognizing or producing a simple complete classification.)

Our set of 'rules' for classifying, chart 7.5, are reproduced here, slightly modified, for quick reference.

CHART 7.5   SUMMARY OF RULES FOR CLASSIFYING

1. Writers must be able to define their class and each member of that class. They should understand the relation of the class and the members to one another and the outside world.
2. A class must have at least two members. If a class has only one member, then that member and the class are the same. In implicit classification some or all members may have to be reconstructed from 'logic' as well as context.
3. In large classes it is not usually necessary nor advisable to state all members. With these and 'infinite' classes, writers must decide which members to list for the readers.

4. All members of a class must have at least one characteristic in common: this commonality is the basis for their all being members of the same class.
5. Each member of a class must be clearly separated from all other members by the basis (bases) for classification which functions to differentiate them from each other.
6. Classification must be made on only one level at a time. Mixing levels is a sure sign of lack of understanding of the principles of classification.

In our experience, students have the most difficulty in giving clear statements of the bases of their classifications. A common error is for the classifier to mix levels of generality and levels for bases of classification (as suggested by rule 2). The following example, handed in by a student, illustrates this type of error.

Classification of houses by types
1. Cape Cod
2. Victorian
3. Tudor
4. French chateau
5. Brick
6. Price range – $50,000 to $80,000

First, of course, the heading is ambiguous: 'types' can mean architectural types (the first four in the list) or can refer to types of construction (number 5). Thus, the classifier has mixed two somewhat related bases. In addition, number 6 gives us a third, quite different basis – that of cost. Also, the two related types are on different levels of generality since we can find one governing the other, depending on just where we begin. That is, the architectural types listed above can be constructed of different materials, thus giving us a class 'Types of architecture' with kinds of construction materials subsumed under each type (for example, Victorian architecture built of brick, of stone, etc.). Or we can have a class 'Materials' with types of architecture subsumed under each of these (for example, stone used for the architectural types Victorian or French chateau, etc.).

Looking again at the list of 'Rules for classifying', we can see that rule 1 poses little problem, especially if the classifier understands the basic concept of formal definition. Rule 3 is an extension of rule 2 and, like rule 2, implies that statements of bases for classification be clear and precise. The first part of rule 4 needs little explanation; the second part, however, can create problems, particularly for those students not trained to reason from a premise.

A good example of the need to apply this kind of reasoning is in paragraph 2 of example 7.10B, p. 92, which illustrates implicit classification. In paragraph 1 both members of the class 'Water reserves' are given, although not in precisely the terms used to name the members of the class. We have the statement, 'Underground water reserves are much larger than those on the surface.' From this it is not difficult for a reader to abstract a class 'Water reserves' and the two members of that class, 'Underground and surface water reserves', by a simple interpretation of the pronoun 'those'. In paragraph 2, however, the major class 'Water' is not stated but only implied by the phrase '... like the pure water defined by chemists.' When this member of the class 'Water' becomes a class in its own right it appears to violate the rule that all classes must have more than one member. To get around this apparent violation the reader needs to infer that there can be other types of 'man-made water' just as there is more than one type of natural water. (While it can be useful for academic students to be able to abstract this kind of implicit information from their reading, whether the teacher should spend much time on exercises that deal with it – analyses of paragraphs, for example – is really a function of the language levels in the class. For those whose ability to read English is, at this point in their work, still uncertain, the struggle can be far too great to make analyses worthwhile, while for those whose reading ability is close to what it should be such work can be profitable.)

As rule 3 is stated in chart 7.5, it is over-simplified. Obviously in working with open-ended (infinite) classes the classifier could not perform the impossible and state all members. The rule really applies to closed classes that contain more members than those the classifier may wish to deal with, or more than necessary for transmitting all of the information required by a reader. For example, if a writer is comparing and contrasting vertebrate and invertebrate animals classification is an excellent framework for making the points clearly and concisely. However, for a writer to try to list all (or even the majority) of the members of each class would be an exercise in futility as well as unnecessary. Giving a few representative members of a class is usually sufficient for most discussions.

Rule 6 has been discussed above in connection with rule 2, to which it is closely related.

A sample classification assignment is given in chart 10.4. The assignment on implicit classification is best thought of as optional. Whether it (or one of the same type) is to be used should depend on the level of the class (for example, lower-intermediate non-native students usually have difficulty in reading well enough to find implied information).

CHART 10.4   SAMPLE INDIVIDUALIZED ASSIGNMENT:
CLASSIFICATION

> From your subject-matter reading, find examples of the following
> types of paragraphs:

1. Find a paragraph that has a statement of classification as its core generalization. This paragraph should be expanded by description and should use the rhetorical technique of causality and result of or comparison and/or contrast.
2. Find a paragraph that develops a complete classification but that does *not* have the statement of classification as its core. This paragraph should be developed by description but it should not use the same rhetorical technique as your first example.
3. Find a paragraph that develops a partial classification. The statement of classification can be, but need not be, the core. The paragraph can be developed by any means.
4. Find a paragraph that contains an implicit classification. Show what the classification elements are by putting a classification diagram beneath your example paragraph.

The grammatical element related to classification that may cause some problems is the same as that in definition – the relative – and the same types of exercises can be used. In fact, statements of classification lend themselves to expansion into paragraphs even more easily than do single-sentence definitions.

Partition

Although not considered a rhetorical function, partition is so often confused with classification (and not only by the non-native learner) that it is worth looking at it in some detail. By definition partition is the process of breaking something into its component parts and naming each. Expanded partition not only names but it describes. In technical discourse, partition is usually applied to physical objects, although anything with parts may be partitioned – a complex concept, a syllogism, etc. While in technical discourse it is functionally most often a part of physical description, because of the tendency to confuse it with classification partition is best discussed by contrasting it with classification rather than introducing it with physical description. This contrast is best made only *after* the students have shown that they understand the basic ideas in the rhetoric of classification.

The confusion between classification and partition is usually due to an uninformed reader assuming that to list under a name (class) what seem to be its parts is breaking it down. However, the 'parts' of a classification (the members/items) are whole units capable of becoming classes themselves. Together they do not add up to a single unit of which each member forms one piece. To state this in other terms, the total number of items listed under a class does not add up to be that class; rather, each member of a class is a specific case of that class. (The technical student might visualize the concept more easily if the teacher equates 'class' with 'set' and 'member' with 'subset'.)

Partition, in contrast, takes a whole (a class or a member of a class) and separates it into its components, many of which cannot function by themselves but must be integrated with other 'parts' to be able to do so. An example that shows the confusion of classifying and partitioning can be seen in the discussion of a chemical compound. A compound is made up of two or more 'wholes' (usually elements) that by uniting become a new 'whole'. For example, forms of the elements sodium and chlorine come together to form salt. To list the forms of these two elements under the heading 'salt' or 'sodium chloride' is partitioning; to take the term 'salt' and list under it the several kinds – underground (mined) salt, sea salt, etc. – is classifying. In brief, sodium and chlorine are not types of salt; they are components of salt. Underground salt and sea salt are types of salt; they are specific examples of the general class we call 'salt'.

A simple way to demonstrate to the students the basic difference between partition and classification is to bring to the classroom two (or three or more) items such as different types of pens (ballpoint, felt tip, etc.), one of which can be easily taken apart. By pointing out that the pens are members of the class 'pens' and then by taking apart one pen and showing as well as listing these parts, the teacher can make a clear contrast between classification and partition.

10.6.4 Instructions

The discussions of the two types of instructions and of instructional information are in chapter 3, sub-section 3.2.3 and chapter 7, section 7.5. Chart 7.6, p. 97, lists the kinds of information given by a set of instructions and, again, is a useful tool to use as a basis for preliminary discussion and as a reference for the students to put in their files.

In teaching the rhetoric of instructions we find it of major importance to make clear the difference between instructions *per se* – both direct and indirect instructions – and instructional information. Because instructional information is so often woven into the instructional statements themselves, students have a tendency to ignore it and to 'get on with the activity' or to misunderstand its function and so skip over it in a kind of frustration.

Similarly, it is important to have the students recognize an indirect instruction as an actual imperative even though the grammatical form is usually passive or modal, or a combination of the two. This problem is most successfully attacked through a discussion of the specialized meanings (in many indirect instructions) of the modals 'should', 'may', and 'can'.

It is important that in teaching the rhetoric of instructions the two types of instructions and instructional information are taught together rather than separately (as suggested for the three rhetorical functions already discussed). One reason for using this approach is the need to distinguish very early the different kinds of information – not always an easy task since they very frequently occur in the same piece of discourse. A second reason is that we have few examples of instructions that are meaningful to academic students. Leaving aside those instructions that accompany problems and exercises in textbooks (for example, 'You have been given an electric light bulb, a socket, some wire, and some insulating tape. Draw a circuit diagram of the system you would put together'), the only 'real world' sources for sets of instructions in academic situations are the manuals used in science and engineering laboratories; that is, the manuals that have been made to accompany the instrumentation purchased for use in such laboratories (for example, oscilloscopes, microscopes, sophisticated measuring devices, etc.). This does *not* include those manuals prepared by processors for specific courses. These are usually edited and so seldom contain the same faults as 'real world' manuals.

Since there is a lack of source materials easily available to the students, it is sometimes necessary to provide them with examples (labeled and unlabeled) from outside their subject-matter areas and, unfortunately, also often outside their experience. To help overcome any feeling on the part of the students that these examples do not represent the 'real world' we try to choose material that at least one student can understand and to hold more in-class workshops in place of some of the individualized assignments, thus letting all students share the knowledge of the one (or more) whose field is being exemplified.

When transferring the learning process from reading to writing, we have the students work back and forth, changing direct into indirect instructions and vice versa, and separating out instructional information from the instructions themselves and putting this information into separate paragraphs by adding language and changing structures as necessary. Since instructions are often found in conjunction with visuals, exercises using both rhetorical functions together are also practical. These are discussed in the sub-section on visuals below.

Chart 10.5 shows an individualized assignment on the rhetoric of instructions. It is designed to be used after the basic discussion on the types of instructions but before the related grammatical elements are introduced.

CHART IO.5   SAMPLE INDIVIDUALIZED ASSIGNMENT:
INSTRUCTIONS

> In your subject-matter reading, find examples of the following sets of instructions:
> 1. a set of direct instructions without any accompanying indirect instructions or instructional information;

2. a set of instructions containing both direct and indirect instructions but not containing any instructional information;
3. a set of instructions containing direct and indirect instructions and instructional information;
4. a set of instructions made up of indirect instructions and instructional information but without any direct instructions.

In bringing in the grammatical elements related to the rhetoric of instructions, as noted above, it is a useful procedure to bring the special meanings of some of the modals into the general discussion on indirect instructions. The ways the definite article is used (and abused) in instructions can either be brought early into the discussion or it can be left until later and treated separately or, because of its difficulty for the non-native student, be brought into initial discussions and treated separately as well. However the teacher chooses to handle the definite article, as much time as can be spared should be allowed for it.

Sets of instructions bring into focus the two lexical problems of subtechnical vocabulary and noun compounds. First, as noted in the comment for example 7.1, writers assume that the reader knows the specialized meanings of the sub-technical words and compounds used; and second, writers tend to change the function of a word or use a word (or the words making up a noun compound) with meanings not in any dictionary (and possibly never to be in a dictionary because only by that writer and only in that document do we find the word, or words, used in that particular way).

10.6.5 *Visual–verbal relationships*

The rhetoric of visual–verbal relationships is discussed briefly in chapter 3, sub-section 3.2.3 and more fully in chapter 7, section 7.6. Chart 7.7, pp. 103–4, summarizes the information the reader should receive from the text accompanying a visual, and chart 7.8, p. 104, provides a 'rule of thumb' for the writer to use when locating a visual in relation to its text. These lists are best used at different times during the discussion of the visual–verbal relationships rather than introduced all at once. The text information summarized in chart 7.7 provides a sound basis for beginning the discussion; the 'Rules for placement of visuals' can then be saved until the discussion dealing with placement is reached. Since this is a problem of production rather than of reading, this topic most often comes up in relation to assignments in which the students are asked to write the text for visuals or to roughly sketch visuals to fit given texts and, in both cases, to state where they would place the visuals in relation to the texts and to justify their placements.

It is not the purpose of the English teacher to train the non-native (or native) reader in understanding the more difficult visuals, such as schematics, flow charts, some types of graphs, etc. That task should be left to the teachers of the technical courses where such visuals are studied and sometimes produced. The concern of English teachers, is the information that a visual plus its text gives the reader and what the physical (locational) relationships of the visual and text should be. (This helps readers locate visuals and it helps writers determine where to locate them.) Chart 7.7 provides the first and chart 7.8, the second.

As we can see from the discussion of the examples in section 7.6, a major value of teaching the rhetoric of visual–verbal relationships is that a piece of text and its visual between them illustrate many of the rhetorical techniques and all of the other rhetorical functions, thus providing a kind of general revision along with new information. Looking at example 7.15 again, we can see that the text begins with a definition by function (although not stated precisely in defining terms) and goes on to give us physical and function description, classification on two levels, and partition. The visual also gives us partition by illustrating some of the named parts. Examples 7.16, p. 108, and 7.17, p. 109, illustrate one way in which sets of instructions (indirect in example 7.16; direct in example 7.17) can be clarified by a related visual. Such texts and their visuals also use causality and result, time order (especially in a set of instructions), and space order (with stress on spatial relationships). In addition, visuals are, by the nature of their function in the discourse, examples of what is being described in their accompanying texts.

Chart 10.6 illustrates an apparently simple individualized assignment for visual–verbal relationships. However, the assignment can be difficult for those students whose fields of study contain few visuals. We usually suggest that these students go to a related field or to a 'hobby', if the discourse for either should contain more visuals than their own subject-matter areas. If this approach fails, the students can be given several sample paragraphs with instructions to choose the required examples from them and then to make detailed analyses.

CHART 10.6   SAMPLE INDIVIDUALIZED ASSIGNMENT:
VISUAL–VERBAL RELATIONSHIPS

> Find examples of the following types of visuals and their texts:
> 1. a visual with a text that explains the development of the visual (that is, discusses the gathering and use of the data the visual is based on);
> 2. a visual that has its text in the caption that is part of the visual;
> 3. a visual with its text incorporated in it;
> 4. a text that contains all four pieces of 'text information'. Identify each clearly in your analysis.

159

The grammatical problems found with description and instructions are also present in the texts that accompany visuals as these texts are simply discourse units expressing one or more of the rhetorical functions. A brief example is the text of example 7.18, pp. 110–11, which illustrates inconsistent use of the definite article along with unwieldly strings of noun compounds.

In addition to discussion of these particular problems, the shifts in tense that occur in the texts of visuals should be pointed out and commented on. As noted in chapter 8, sub-section 8.5.2, there is more of the 'temporal' element in tense shift in texts accompanying visuals than there is in such shifts in passages of description: gathering data and creating the visual are described in the past tense because these operations are over and done with. The reference to the visual itself, telling the reader when to look at it, is in the present tense as is the discussion that tells the reader what to look for and why this particular information is important. From the readers' point of view it is 'time now' when they are asked to look at and read about the visual, thus the temporal factor is definitely involved in the writer's choice of tense.

Visual–verbal relationships are a very useful tool to exploit when teaching reading or when transferring the teaching emphasis to writing. For reading, modified individualized assignments work very well: the students are asked to bring examples of texts and visuals that illustrate the various rhetorical features – perhaps those that need to be studied further – these are examples accompanied by analyses focusing on paragraph structure, rhetorical techniques used, and rhetorical functions chosen, along with a discussion of how well the sample text fulfills the conditions laid down in charts 7.7 and 7.8. (The difficulty with this type of assignment is that complex visuals are troublesome to reproduce unless photocopying equipment is available and affordable. In cases where it is not, students can be asked to bring either a) a rough sketch indicating the main points of the visual or b) a description of the visual.)

When the students are ready for writing, the number of possible exercises is limited only by the time available. In addition to the exercises relating to the placement of visuals discussed above, students can be asked to make the texts accompanying their visuals define or classify or describe, etc., or they can be asked to design a visual that would require a text to perform one or more of the rhetorical functions and/or rhetorical techniques. In asking for a visual to be designed, the teacher can expect a good deal of rough work (although engineering students on the whole seem quite capable artists). The quality of a visual obviously should not be our concern; but however rough, the visual should give us the information we need so that it plus the accompanying text add up to a meaningful unit of discourse.

At this stage very useful – and often interesting – exercises can be developed around having the students work in pairs or, if the situation is favorable, having them work in larger groups. Whether we are dealing with pairs of students or groups of three or four, we try to avoid having any two students who share the same native language work together, thus requiring them to discuss their work in English. In those cases where the students are all from the same country (or if we are teaching in a non-English-speaking country) we try to group the students according to their ability in English; that is, where possible we avoid putting together students whose levels of English vary too greatly. (The result of having a 'good' student in with less qualified students is usually that the 'good' student does most of the work!)

Once we have pairs, or groups, we can assign several exercises. For example, we ask one student to prepare (or choose from a printed source) a visual. The other student (or other members of the group) then writes a caption and a text to go with the visual. The first student then determines the placement of the visual in relation to the text. If we are working with pairs, we have the students reverse their roles; if we are working with groups, we have each member in turn choose a visual and, once the text is written, determine placement. Work of this type can be done in workshops or, with residential students, as outside assignments. The latter, however, can carry the danger of having assistance provided by a native speaker.

10.7   Teaching the rhetorical–grammatical relationships

The rhetorical–grammatical relationships are discussed in detail in chapter 8 and are also noted above in the pertinent sub-sections on teaching the rhetorical functions. If we have treated the related grammar when we presented each rhetorical function as suggested above in sub-section 10.6.1, then at this stage we need bring in only those grammatical points the students did not fully understand. If we have followed the alternative procedure suggested (also in sub-section 10.6.1), then we should devote some time to each of the grammatical elements discussed briefly with the discussions of the rhetorical functions. How much time should be spent on each grammatical point is, of course, determined by how well the students seemed to understand the point when it was made in conjunction with its related rhetorical function. As a generalization, I can say that the passive–stative distinction is usually grasped quite quickly, as is the non-temporal use of tense in description and in visual-–verbal relationships. The definite article, on the other hand, remains a problem that many students never seem to solve, and we have often given it more than one extra class hour.

Chart 10.7 is a composite sample individualized assignment for the rhetorical–grammatical relationships. Depending on when the discussion of a given grammatical element takes place, this assignment may be broken into several parts and used during the study of a particular function. (The reason for the assignment being so long is given in the comments in square brackets at the end of the chart.)

CHART 10.7   SAMPLE INDIVIDUALIZED ASSIGNMENT:
RHETORICAL– GRAMMATICAL RELATIONSHIPS

In your subject-matter reading find examples of the following:
1. Find a paragraph of description that uses mostly stative verb forms.
2. Find a paragraph of description that uses mostly passive verb forms.
3. Find a set of instructions which 'misuses' the definite article either by omitting it when it should be used or by using it when the 'rules' say that another form of the article (the indefinite article or zero article) should be used.
4. Find a set of instructions that illustrates the 'special' uses of the modal 'should'. If possible, your paragraph should also contain the special uses of 'can' and/or 'may'.
(Suggestion: For sets of instructions look at some of the manuals in engineering or science laboratories, especially those written to accompany purchased laboratory equipment.)
5. Find a paragraph of description that uses mostly the present tense.
6. Find a paragraph of description that uses mostly the past tense.
7. Find a text that uses the past tense to explain how the data was gathered for the visual that the text relates to and also how the data was used to make the visual.
8. Find a text that uses the present tense when telling the reader to look at the visual and when discussing its relationship to the subject being illustrated by the visual. (Your texts can be attached to or separate from their visuals.)

[Because we are working here with the relationships between the grammatical elements and the rhetorical functions, there is overlap with some of the previous individualized assignments. This suggests that if we introduce the grammatical element(s) relating to a particular function during the discussion of that function we can also use some of the individualized grammatical assignments with (or immediately after) we give out the assignment for the function being studied. For that reason we have made the above sample assignment fairly inclusive so that the separate parts can be used with the rhetorical function assignments if so desired.]

Following the final presentation of the grammatical elements we find it fruitful to pause and check to make certain that not only have the various parts of the process been understood but that their integration is understood as well: that the students see, let us say, the relationships between definition and classification; that they grasp the relationship between instructional information and instructions themselves, and that they see how text and visual work together.

10.8   Teaching the lexical elements

Above I suggested that we stop and check the students' grasp of the rhetorical process even though it has not been completely presented. Although we find the lexical problems discussed in chapter 9 tied in with the several rhetorical techniques and functions, they were not included above primarily because they are sufficiently different to need a separate discussion.

The sub-technical vocabulary can be covered fairly quickly, especially if students have access to specialist dictionaries (that is, scientific and technical dictionaries, both mono- and bilingual). Once learners realize that many 'common' words in general English have specialized meanings in their particular scientific or technical field, they usually have a minimum of trouble with the sub-technical lexis.

Compounds, however, are a more difficult problem. It is often useful to cull the students' individualized assignments for compounds that can be presented to the class as a whole for analysis and discussion. As noted in chapter 9, the more complex and very complex types of compounds are best left out of teaching plans, except, perhaps, for a few demonstrations of their difficulty, leaving the translations of these to the technical course teacher. Practice in making analyses of simple and complex compounds is useful as a basis both for understanding and for producing compounds at these levels.

A compounding exercise that helps students improve their reading is to have them create compounds of varying levels of complexity. To prepare exercises of this type may require the aid of a technical colleague as it consists of giving the students lists of words from their own fields and having them make, for example, several two-word and several three-word compounds. This we find to be an excellent way of making clear to the students the difference between headword (or head group) and modifiers. The compounds thus made can also be used as bases for an additional writing exercise: the students are asked to take their most complex compounds and put them in discourse contexts, writing paragraphs of definition (and, if feasible, paragraphs of classification and/or description), using the compounds as the focal points of these paragraphs.

Chart 10.8 illustrates an individualized lexical assignment. The time required for this assignment is rather lengthy as it has two sections which are usually handed out about a week apart. While the first section could be given by itself, without the follow-up second assignment the students would gain little more than practice in using a dictionary. It is our experience that both parts are necessary if the assignment is to be of much help to the students.

CHART 10.8   SAMPLE INDIVIDUALIZED ASSIGNMENT:
LEXICAL WORK

Assignment I
From your subject-matter reading find the following terms:
1. Find five nouns whose meanings you either do not know or are uncertain of.
2. Find three sub-technical terms; that is, terms whose common meanings (usually the first meaning given in a general English dictionary) do not fit the context in which you find the term.
3. Find six noun compounds, at least two of which are three-word compounds and the remainder are two-word compounds.
4. Note: This part of the assignment is *not* required. Find up to five four-word (or longer) compounds.

Instructions. Do the following for each term that you find:
1. Find the general dictionary definition of the term, choosing the meaning closest to your field of study (for example, if your field is biology but the dictionary does not give a 'biology' but does give a 'botany' meaning, then choose this).
2. If there is a technical dictionary (an all-English, not a bilingual, dictionary) in your field, copy from it the definition of your term that seems best to fit the context you found the word in.
3. Write the context in which you found the word. Write at least one sentence; write more than one sentence if that is necessary to clarify the meaning of your term.

[Note to the teacher: Assume that the students have turned in their lists of terms and that these have been gone through and that two terms from each of the first three categories have been marked. The assignments are then returned to the students with the following instructions.]

Assignment II
1. Choose one of the underlined terms from each of the first three categories. Using the definitions you have copied from dictionaries, write the following:
    a) a paragraph that uses your definition as the core statement in the form of a formal definition and that is expanded by explication;
    b) a paragraph that uses your definition as the core statement (again in the form of a formal definition) and is expanded by description or classification;

164

    c) a paragraph with your defined term as the core statement in the form of a semi-formal definition and with the type of expansion the one that you feel to be best.

2. Using the other underlined term from each of the three categories, repeat the assignment given above but with the following changes:
   a) one of your definitions is to be semi-formal and the other two non-formal;
   b) your definitions can be the core statements of your paragraphs but need not be;
   c) each of the paragraphs can be expanded by whichever way you think best.

10.9   Controlling writing assignments

If writing beyond the level of practice paragraphs is a goal of the course, we need to take into consideration the way in which we can direct and control writing assignments. In fact, even if we are limiting writing to the paragraph, certain problems need to be looked at.

In a class in which the students are given marks, they are sometimes tempted to improve these by having native speakers (if available) write (or help write) out-of-class assignments. As a rule teachers can tell whether the assignment written out of class is the work of non-native or native students since each tends to make different types of errors. If, on the other hand, assignments are to be done in the class then too high a proportion of time that might well be used in discussion is being taken up by workshops. One solution to this problem is for the teacher to decide how much time can be given to workshops and then either tailor the writing assignments to fit this amount of time or save the time for in-class revision of outside assignments. For example, if students are bringing in work that has obviously received outside help, they can be asked to write similar paragraphs in class.

We put writing assignments into the three general categories of controlled, semi-controlled, and uncontrolled, depending on how much time the teacher spends with the students while they are writing. Here, I am referring to writing assignments beyond the paragraph in length: assignments, for instance, such as the term paper or the end-of-term essay. The primary purpose of these assignments is not to determine the depth of the students' knowledge on certain topics but to determine how well they can integrate the rhetorical, grammatical, and lexical concepts that they have learned. Hopefully, they can put this knowledge into a coherent piece of prose that also manages to say something in relation to their subject-matter interests.

Teaching the rhetorical process

The uncontrolled assignment

An uncontrolled assignment is exactly what it sounds like: the students are turned loose and told to write a paper and to hand this paper in at a given time. This procedure is related to the individualization concept only in that the students have to choose topics within the limits of their fields of study or of interest. Papers of this type are usually judged only on the final result; thus the obvious danger that someone with a greater knowledge of English may help write, or may edit, the paper.

The semi-controlled assignment

A semi-controlled assignment is individualized in that the students choose their own topics (often from a list prepared by the teacher) and they choose their sources and select data from these sources with little, if any, outside assistance. Using this data, the students write their own initial drafts. Control is exercised by the teacher vetting the topics once they are chosen and by requiring information in advance: an outline or an abstract or both at different times during the writing process. By vetting the topics chosen and by requiring an outline and/or an abstract, teachers can avoid situations such as being given papers from postgraduates (or even advanced undergraduates) written originally for their technical classes. While such papers may contain as many non-native errors as those written on a lower technical level (or even more errors than usual as the students wrestle with involved concepts), for the majority of English teachers, trying to correct them can (and usually does) mean that numerous errors will be missed. [This may sound nonsensical, but not having a 'deep' enough background in a subject can cause a teacher to overlook a 'misused' preposition – 'to' may sound as logical in a given place as, say, 'for'; a non-defining relative may appear perfectly acceptable when a defining relative is required, etc.]

Some students may be qualified in terms of subject-matter knowledge to write about highly technical topics (even though they may not be so qualified in terms of writing acceptable English), but the majority of students in the undergraduate classroom will hardly have the same subject-matter knowledge to draw on. By vetting the topic and requiring an outline or abstract (even if it is only a preliminary one), teachers can keep the students from trying to write papers too ambitious in terms of topic. They can also control to a degree the length of the papers, thus avoiding the all too common problem of students working in areas that require far more writing than they have been assigned or, for that matter, have the time for.

Assuming that the topic and its length are under control and that checking the outline and abstract have resulted in guidance in organization and content, the teacher may still find it expedient to have a draft of

166

the paper written under supervision and corrected before the final paper is attempted. Despite the precautions listed above, many teachers will find themselves faced with papers that are beyond their knowledge of a subject, as even teachers with some science background cannot be expected to have an in-depth knowledge of all the subject areas represented by their students. The solution to this problem is to ask a colleague in science or technology for help whenever there is a suspicion that an error might have been overlooked because of the reader's lack of comprehension of the subject matter. (We have more than once been surprised to find how pleased many Engineering College colleagues are to parade their knowledge before a teacher of English, especially when that knowledge relates to bits of 'grammar'.)

The controlled assignment

The completely controlled assignment allows the students minimal freedom to work on their own by monitoring virtually every step in the writing process. Unfortunately it uses a good deal of class time. It does not, as might seem the case, take away the element of individualization of the assignment as the students are still working in their own subject-matter areas and at their own levels of language ability. Among the advantages are those of control of topic, of organization and of the actual use of the data gathered, along with guidance of the writing itself, from the preliminary through the final draft. Every step taken by the student in the writing process is under supervision except that of actually gathering the data (in addition to libraries, sources for technical papers are most often laboratories, field studies, and information from 'experts'). A step-by-step procedure for controlling writing assignments to the extent given here is in chart 10.9. This is a combination of a suggested handout for the students and a set of comments for the guidance of the teacher. These comments have been put in square brackets.[1]

CHART 10.9   PROCEDURE FOR WRITING ASSIGNMENTS

1. Submit your topic for approval; include a brief statement as to the depth of coverage planned and the probable length of the work. If feasible at this stage, you should also submit some possible sources.

[The topics can come either directly from the student or can be from a list developed by the teacher. For lower-level classes (lower in the sense of subject-matter training and/or of ability in English), the second procedure is recommended. Should there be difficulty in preparing a list, a useful technique is to have the students suggest titles; another is to go to those teachers who represent the subject-matter areas of the students and ask for topics. (The danger here is that this list may end up containing topics beyond the students' abilities.)]

2. Once your topic is approved, find your main sources for data (if you have not already done so) and do some preliminary reading. (An encyclopedia is often useful at this stage in your research.)

   From this preliminary reading, make an outline that shows your main topics, main sub-topics, and such detail as you may have in mind at this point. Be sure that the outline reveals your organizational pattern and shows that you plan to use as many of the rhetorical functions as your topic allows, and where in the paper you plan to put these. (Unless your paper calls for *instructions*, this function will probably not be represented. However, all of the other functions we have studied should be used as often as possible within the logic of the paper.) When this outline is returned to you, revise it on the basis of suggestions and corrections made and resubmit it.

   Include with the outline the sources you used to prepare it. Be sure that the information on your sources is complete. Add any possible additional sources you plan to use (or that you think you might use).

[The outline is the first real control point. Although checking it (sometimes two and three times) is time consuming, making sure that the students have sound outlines to work from can save time later. This is also a good place to check the submitted list of sources – for completeness and to determine if some students have chosen sources too difficult to comprehend.]

3. Once the outline is approved, go to the sources you have listed and get your data down on paper. You may use any form you wish (note form, outline form, etc.) to record the data. But please make sure that your handwriting is legible! (If your original notes have been scribbled or written in a hurry, copy them before handing them in.) The source for each piece of data must be shown with that data. If you are asked to make additions (such as getting more information on a given area), do so as quickly as possible so that your work will not be out of step with the rest of the group.

[The data, like the outline and the sources, may need modifying before the students can use it in papers written at the levels we are concerned with here. In our experience, the greatest problems with data gathered by students are: 1. They gather much more data than they can use. 2. They do not differentiate between generalizations and the specific supporting information for the generalizations. This leads to uneven organization as well as overloads of data in their papers. 3. Despite all of the teacher's efforts, students will gather data far too technical for the level of their paper.]

4.   When your data is returned, you will be asked to use it to write a preliminary draft of your paper. This writing will be done in the classroom under supervision. If the drafts cannot be finished in one class session, the papers will be collected and returned to be finished at the next meeting. No work done outside and brought to the class will be accepted.

[It is possible, of course, for the students to take their drafts away – once these have been gone over and marked for errors and other weaknesses – and revise them. However, this defeats the purpose of the controlled assignment – total supervision. To be sure of complete control, the teacher should make certain that step 5 is followed.]

5.   You will continue to write in class, under supervision, until your paper is acceptable in terms of your use of English as well as of organization and content. When you submit the final version, it must also include your sources put in formal bibliographic form. You should also include your preliminary draft(s), outline(s) and the data you worked from.

[If step 5 is not followed and revisions are made outside the classroom, then all data, drafts, etc. should be submitted with the final version. There are two advantages to this compromise: 1. It leaves more time in class for other matters. 2. It may reach you in a much more readable condition than it would if written wholly in the class – it may even be typewritten! It is also possible to accept a final paper and then have the student take it away and recopy it so that it will be more legible.

Whichever procedure is followed, the teacher should always keep as many drafts, notes, etc. as possible. Only that material the student needs to do a final draft and that the teacher wants in 'readable' form shoud be taken out of the classroom.]

The advantages to be gained from exercising as much control over writing assignments as time permits can be summarized as follows:
1.   It teaches the students research techniques and stresses the importance of logical organization of data.
2.   It helps students learn to select from a mass of data and it helps them understand the difference between a generalization and its specific support (which, of course, carries them directly back to the rhetoric of the paragraph and core statements).
3.   It is, in a sense, a review of the entire rhetorical process since under supervision the students can be directed in using the appropriate

169

rhetorical techniques and rhetorical functions as they develop their papers.

For those teachers working in an English-speaking environment completely controlling a writing assignment provides an additional advantage: it prevents students having their papers revised (or edited – or even written) by a native speaker of English. I have heard teachers say that their students would *never* do such a thing! Perhaps not, but our experience (along with that of a good many other EST teachers we have spoken to) is that some students can be tempted to improve their class standing by having native-speaker assistance with outside writing assignments. (This is especially true in those classes in which term marks are given.) As a rule, experienced teachers can tell whether assignments written outside class are the work of non-native or native students since each tends to make different types of errors. If there is a suspicion that some students are bringing in work that has received outside help (and this can often occur with early assignments as well as with the later ones), having similar paragraphs written in class quickly shows up tell-tale differences.

10.10 Conclusion

As we learned early in our work, the most valuable element in teaching the rhetorical process is the example. Both labeled and unlabeled examples not only provide a basis for discussion and for checking student progress, they also give the students something concrete to take from the class; something that they can study in their own time and can use when they are reviewing for examinations or use when preparing papers, whether for the English class or for other courses at a later date.

In this book, as many examples have been included as space has allowed. Most have been classroom tested and can still be used whether they are 'timely' or not. As pointed out in chapter 2, section 2.2, not all of the examples chosen are 'current', nor are there many designed strictly for use with students in one particular field of science or technology; thus, most of them can be used when applying the teaching procedure we have called 'parallelism' (chapter 4, section 4.4).

Notes

Chapter 1 Introduction

1. When our program started, Larry Selinker was a member of the University of Washington Department of Linguistics and Director of the English as a Second Language program. Until recently he was Director of the English Language Institute and Professor of Linguistics at the University of Michigan, Ann Arbor. Recently he has given up the post of Director in order to devote his time and energy to teaching and research in linguistics.
2. At the time referred to, John Lackstrom was a graduate student in linguistics at the University of Washington. Formerly Director of The Intensive English Institute, and Associate Professor in the Department of Linguistics, Utah State University, Logan, Utah, he is currently Professor of Linguistics at the same institution.
3. Robert Bley-Vroman, also a graduate student in linguistics at the University of Washington, has been Director of Studies at the English Language Institute of the University of Michigan and is presently a member of the Department of Linguistics at the University of Texas, Austin. He and Larry Selinker are currently working together on language research.
4. While Thomas Huckin came somewhat later into the program (also as a graduate student in Linguistics at the University of Washington), he contributed equally to its development. Although taking his postgraduate degrees in linguistics, Dr Huckin turned his efforts to research in scientific and technical English and to teaching it to both native and foreign engineering students. Until recently at the University of Michigan, he is now Associate Professor at Carnegie–Mellon University in Pittsburgh, Pennsylvania.

Chapter 3 The rhetoric of EST discourse

1. The best source for information on organization of technical material and for information on headings and sub-headings is a good technical writing book. Those we have found most helpful are listed in 'Further reading'.
2. For the term 'core' we are indebted to Emeritus Professors J. W. Souther and M. L. White of the Humanistic–Social Studies Department of the College of Engineering, University of Washington (Seattle). As far as we have been able to determine, they introduced the term in the 1950s while lecturing on technical writing to a group of professional engineers.
3. The basic work on this way of categorizing the rhetorical techniques was also done by Professors Souther and White. This concept of patterns – natural and

logical − as applied to the relating and developing of ideas in written EST discourse was first published in J. W. Souther, *Technical Report Writing* (New York, Wylie, 1957), pp. 33–5, and refined in J. W. Souther and M. L. White, *Technical Report Writing*, second edition (New York, Wylie, 1977), pp. 39–40.

4. When the term 'paragraph' is used without qualification (such as 'physical' or 'conceptual' paragraph), *conceptual* paragraph is to be understood.

Chapter 4   The individualizing process

1. For a somewhat different approach to 'parallelism' see Henry Widdowson on 'gradual approximation': in 'The Communicative Approach and its Application', *English for Specific Purposes: An International Seminar* (The British Council, Bogotá, Colombia, 17–22 April 1977), pp. 23–33; and in 'Gradual Approximation', *Explorations in Applied Linguistics* (Oxford University Press, 1979), pp. 75–88.

2. Although the subject may seem a quite different one, the techniques used in the 'simulation' approach to this type of teaching are often quite closely related. The relationships between simulation and the use of 'genuine' materials (and, to a lesser extent, the other types of materials discussed) can be seen in Ken Jones's discussion of 'simulation': particularly pp. 4–15 in Ken Jones, *Simulations in Language Teaching* (New Directions in Language Teaching, Cambridge University Press, 1982), where he provides this definition 'A simulation is reality of function in a simulated and structured environment', and then goes on to relate simulations to language, communication skills, motivation, and realism. We might point out here that the individualized approach is in large part a simulation technique in that it provides a simulated, structured environment for an approach whose essence is 'reality'.

3. The copyright law allows a reader to make a single copy of part of a book (or other publication) for purposes of private study. We can say, then, that in general the students may make single copies of short excerpts from their subject-matter reading; however, it is always safest to check the local position on copyright before allowing the students to photocopy any copyrighted materials. Further, the law does *not* allow the making of multiple copies of extracts. When the law is scrupulously followed in this regard, 'genuine' materials cannot be made in quantity and handed out but must be copied individually by each student. Thoroughly adapted and synthesized materials should not come under the same restrictions; however, again it is important to check before proceeding.

Chapter 7   The rhetorical functions

1. This analysis was first made by R. Mary Todd Trimble and presented by her in a paper entitled 'Literary Training and the Teaching of EST to Non-Native Speakers' at the Fourth International Congress of Applied Linguistics (AILA), Stuttgart, August 1975. A revised version of the paper was published in

English Teaching Forum, 15 (1977), 11–15, under the title 'Literary Training and the Teaching of Scientific and Technical English'. The original version has been distributed since 1976 by the *ESL Newsletter* published by the English Language Institute, Oregon State University, Corvallis, Oregon.

2. This approach to visuals was first suggested by Professor J. W. Souther in his text, *Technical Report Writing* (see note 3, chapter 3), pp. 39–42. The concept was expanded in the second edition: J. W. Souther and M. L. White, *Technical Report Writing* (see note 3, chapter 3), pp. 42–9.

Chapter 8   Rhetorical–grammatical relationships

1. These modals are discussed in all general reference grammars of English. The following list includes those we have found to be among the most interesting. The order does not indicate priority of any kind; it is alphabetic: L. G. Alexander, W. Stannard Allen, R. A. Close and R. J. O'Neill, *English Grammatical Structure* (London: Longman, 1975), pp. 94ff; P. Christopherson and A. O. Sandved, *An English Grammar* (Basingstoke: Macmillan, 1969), pp. 200ff; R. A. Close, *A Reference Grammar for Students* (London: Longman, 1975), pp. 267ff; R. A. Close, *English as a Foreign Language* (Boston, Mass.: Harvard University Press, 1962), pp. 118–19, revised 1981 and published by Allen and Unwin, London, pp. 118ff; Norman Coe, *A Learner's Grammar of English* (London: Nelson, 1980), pp. 108ff; Sandra McKay and Lisa Rosenthal, *Writing for a Specific Purpose* (Englewood Cliffs, New Jersey: Prentice-Hall, 1980), pp. 102ff; Randolph Quirk, Sidney Greenbaum, Geoffrey Leech and Jan Svartvik, *A Grammar of Contemporary English* (London: Longman, 1972), pp. 100ff.

2. Two EST books that deal with the subject of modals are: J. R. Ewer and G. Latorre, *A Course in Basic Scientific English* (London: Longman, 1969), pp. 73–74 and 91, and John Swales, *Writing Scientific English* (London: Nelson, 1971), pp. 47ff. A useful article covering the use of the modals 'can' and 'may' in EST is by John Lackstrom, 'Teaching Modals in EST Discourse' in *English for Specific Purposes: Science and Technology*, ed. Mary Todd Trimble, Louis Trimble and Karl Drobnic (Corvallis, Oregon: English Language Institute, Oregon State University, 1978), pp. 53–73.

3. Thomas N. Huckin and Leslie A. Olsen, *English for Science and Technology: A Handbook for Non-Native Speakers* (New York: McGraw-Hill, 1983), pp. 429–40.

4. Geoffrey Leech and Jan Svartvik, *A Communicative Grammar of English* (London: Longman, 1975), pp. 131ff.

5. There has not been a great deal of research into the problems non-native speakers have with the English articles, especially the definite article. The most useful recent work has been done by Thomas N. Huckin and Leslie A. Olsen, who devised a new (and successful) method of teaching the articles to non-native students. This is presented in *English for Science and Technology: A Handbook for Non-Native Speakers* (see note 3 above), chapter 18, pp. 367–88. (This chapter was also published in Lary Selinker, Elaine Tarone and Victor Hanzeli, eds, *English for Academic and Technical Purposes* (Rowley,

Mass.: Newbury House, 1981), pp. 165–92. For recent research findings on the definite article (and their application) see, Mary Todd Trimble and Louis Trimble, 'Article Use in Reading Scientific and Technical English Discourse' in J. M. Ulijn and A. K. Pugh, eds., *Reading for Professional Purposes: Methods and Materials in Teaching Languages* (Leuwen: ACCO, 1985). (Note at the end of the paper the section 'References' for additional sources on the definite article and related topics.)

6. This topic appears to have been subjected to even less research than the definite article: to our knowledge, only two articles have appeared since the publication of the initial suggestion in John Lackstrom, Larry Selinker and Louis Trimble, 'Technical Rhetorical Principles and Grammatical Choice', *TESOL Quarterly*, 7 (1973), 127–36. The first of these articles is concerned with the non-temporal use of tense in respect to reference to past research (this is dealt with in chapter 8, sub-section 8.5.3): see Sandra Oster, 'The Uses of Tense in Reporting Past Literature in EST', in Selinker *et al.* (see note 5 above), pp. 76–90. The second is more general and is really a follow-up of the 1973 article by Lackstrom *et al.*, noted above, and of other, later articles dealing with the same topic. See Mary Todd Trimble and Louis Trimble, 'Rhetorical–Grammatical Features of Scientific and Technical Texts as a Major Factor in Written ESP Communication' in *Proceedings of the Third European Symposium on LSP*, ed. Jorgen Hoedt *et al.* (Copenhagen: The LSP Centre, Copenhagen School of Economics, 1982), pp. 199–216.

Chapter 9   Lexical problems in EST discourse

1. Many dictionaries do not list the word 'lexis', although they do give 'lexical', 'lexicographer', etc. Our definition comes from the *Longman Dictionary of Contemporary English* (1978).
2. J. Ronayne Cowan, 'Lexical and Syntactic Research for the Design of EFL Reading Materials', *TESOL Quarterly*, 8 1974, p. 391.
3. An interesting and useful treatment of noun compounds in EST discourse is in Ljerka Bartolic, 'Nominal Compounds in Technical English', *English for Specific Purposes: Science and Technology*, Mary Todd Trimble *et al.*, eds. (see note 2 for chapter 8), pp. 257–77.

Chapter 10   Teaching the rhetorical process

1. Much of the credit for devising this approach to controlling student writing assignments belongs to Dr Elaine Tarone of the Department of Linguistics, University of Minnesota, Minneapolis, Minnesota. She developed her approach while head of the English as a Second Language program at the University of Washington, Seattle.

Further reading

Books

Altman, Howard B. and C. Vaughan James, *Foreign Language Teaching: Meeting Individual Needs*, Pergamon Institute of English, Oxford, Pergamon Press, 1980

British Council, *English for Academic Purposes: An International Seminar*, Bogotá, Colombia, 1977

Close, R., *The Language We Use for Science*, London, Longman, 1975

Davies, Florence and Terry Greene, *Reading for Learning in the Sciences*, Edinburgh, Schools Council/Oliver and Boyd, 1984

Grellet, Françoise, *Developing Reading Skills: A Practical Guide to Reading and Comprehension Exercises*, Cambridge, Cambridge University Press, 1981

Hoedt, Jorgen and Robin Turner, eds., *The World of LSP*, Copenhagen, The LSP Centre, Copenhagen School of Economics, 1981

Hoedt, Jorgen and Robin Turner, eds., *New Bearings in LSP*, Copenhagen, The LSP Centre, Copenhagen School of Economics, 1981

Hoedt, Jorgen, Lita Lundquist, Heribert Picht and Jacques Qvistgaard, eds., *Pragmatics and LSP*, Proceedings of the Third European Symposium on LSP (Copenhagen, 1981), Copenhagen, The LSP Centre, Copenhagen School of Economics, 1982

Holden, Susan, ed., *English for Specific Purposes*, Modern English Publications, 1977

James, Gregory, ed., *The ESP Classroom—Methodology, Materials, Expectations*, SELMOUS Conference Papers, Exeter, University of Exeter Linguistic Studies, 1984

Kennedy, Chris and Rod Bolitho, *English for Specific Purposes*, Essential Language Teaching Series, London, Macmillan, 1984

Littlewood, William, *Communicative Language Teaching: An Introduction*, Cambridge, Cambridge University Press, 1981

Mackay, Ronald and Alan Mountford, eds., *English for Specific Purposes*, London, Longman, 1978

Mackay, Ronald and Joe D. Palmer, eds., *Languages for Specific Purposes: program design and evaluation*, Rowley, Mass., Newbury House, 1981

Mackay, Ronald, Bruce Barkman and R. R. Jordan, eds., *Reading in a Second Language*, Rowley, Mass., Newbury House, 1979

McDonough, Jo, *ESP in Perspective, A Practical Guide*, London, Collins ELT, 1984

Pugh, A. K. and J. M. Ulijn, *Reading for Professional Purposes, Studies and Practices in Native and Foreign Languages*, London, Heinemann Educational Books, 1984

Further reading

Pugh, A. K. and J. M. Ulijn, eds., *Reading for Professional Purposes: Methods and Materials in Teaching Languages*, Leuven, Belgium, ACCO, 1985

Robinson, Pauline, *E.S.P.: The Current Situation*, Oxford, Pergamon Press, 1980

Selinker, Larry, Louis Trimble and Robert Vroman, *Working Papers in English for Science and Technology*, Seattle, Washington, College of Engineering, University of Washington, 1972

Selinker, L., Elaine Tarone and Victor Hanzel, eds., *English for Academic and Technical Purposes: Studies in Honor of Louis Trimble*, Rowley, Mass., Newbury House, 1981

Swales, John and Hassan Mustafa, eds., *English for Specific Purposes in the Arab World*, Birmingham, University of Aston Language Studies Unit, 1984

Todd Trimble, Mary, Louis Trimble and Karl Drobnic, eds., *English for Specific Purposes: Science and Technology*, Corvallis, Oregon, Oregon State University Press, 1978

Widdowson, H. G., *Teaching Language as Communication*, London, Oxford University Press, 1978

Widdowson, H. G., *Explorations in Applied Linguistics*, London, Oxford University Press, 1979

Journals and series containing articles on EST

CILT Reports and Papers, The British Council, London

ELT Documents, The British Council, London

English Language Teaching Journal, Oxford University Press

English Teaching Forum, United States Information Agency, Washington, D.C.

The ESP Journal, American University, Washington, D.C.

ESP Newsletter, Oregon State University, Corvallis, Oregon

ETIC Occasional Papers, The British Council, London

Fachsprache, Wilhelm Braumueller, Vienna

Language Teaching and Linguistics: Abstracts, Cambridge University Press, Cambridge

Reading in a Foreign Language, University of Aston, Birmingham

TESOL Quarterly, Georgetown University, Washington, D.C.

World English, Pergamon Press, Oxford

Journal articles based on the University of Washington EST Program

Larry Selinker, John Lackstrom and Louis Trimble, 'Grammar and Technical English', *English as a Second Language: Current Issues*, ed. Robert C. Lugton, The Center for Curriculum Development, Chilton, 1970, pp. 101–33; reprinted in *English Teaching Forum*, September–October 1972, pp. 3–14; reprinted in *The Art of TESOL*, part 2, *English Teaching Forum*, XIII: 3 and 4 (1975), 250–60

Larry Selinker, John Lackstrom and Louis Trimble 'Technical Rhetorical Principles and Grammatical Choice', *TESOL Quarterly*, VII: 2 (June 1973),

127–36; reprinted in *English Teaching Forum*, September 1973, pp. 1–7; reprinted in *A TEFL Anthology*, United States Information Agency, n.d., pp. 258–63; originally presented as a paper read at the 3rd International Congress of Applied Linguistics [AILA], Copenhagen, Denmark, August 1972

Louis Trimble, 'Sociolinguistics in the ESL Classroom' [in Croatian as 'Sociolingvistika U Razredu'], *Strani Jezici*, University of Zagreb, Yugoslavia, Autumn 1974, pp. 166–73 (translated by Vera Andrassy, Institute of Linguistics, University of Zagreb); originally presented as two lectures at a seminar for Yugoslav teachers of English, Brela, Yugoslavia, October 1973

Larry Selinker, Louis Trimble and Thomas Huckin, 'An Annotated Bibliography of Research in Scientific and Technical Language', *Reports 9, The Yugoslav Serbo-Croatian English Contrastive Project*, Institute of Linguistics, University of Zagreb, Yugoslavia, 1974, pp. 108–18

Larry Selinker and Louis Trimble. 'Formal Written Communication and ESL', *Journal of Technical Writing and Communication*, IV: 2 (Spring 1974), 81–91; reprinted in *English Teaching Forum*, XIV: 4 (1976), 22–6 as 'Scientific and Technical Writing: The Choice of Tense'; this latter version reprinted in *A TEFL Anthology*, United States Information Agency, n.d., pp. 269–73; originally presented as a paper read at the Annual Conference of the TESOL Organization, San Juan, Puerto Rico, May 1973

Larry Selinker, Louis Trimble and Robert Bley-Vroman, 'Presupposition and Technical Rhetoric', *English Language Teaching Journal* (U.K.), October 1974, pp. 61–5; an earlier draft published in *The Trend in Engineering* (University of Washington, Seattle), XXV:2 (April 1973), 22–5

Larry Selinker, Mary Todd Trimble and Louis Trimble, 'Presuppositional Rhetorical Information in EST Discourse', *TESOL Quarterly*, X:3 (September 1976), 281–90; originally presented as a paper read at the 4th International Congress of Applied Linguistics [ALIA], Stuttgart, West Germany, August 1975

Louis Trimble, 'An Approach to Reading Scientific and Technical English' [in Croatian as 'Primjena Znanstveno-Strucne Komunikacije U Nastavi Citanja'], *Strano Jezici*, IV:3 (1975), 183–7 (translator not known); revised and reprinted in *Lenguas para Objetivos Especificos*, Cuaderno 4 (1977): in English, pp. 1–15, in Spanish, pp. 16–30 (a special volume of the journal *EDUTEC*, Universidad Autonoma Metropolitana, Mexico City, Mexico); revised version reprinted in *English Teaching Forum*, XVII:4 (October 1979), 2–5, 21; originally a paper presented at a joint meeting of the International Association of Teachers of English as a Foreign Language (IATEFL) and the Hungarian Academy of Sciences (TIT) Budapest, Hungary, April 1974

Mary Todd Trimble and Louis Trimble, 'Literary Training and the Teaching of Scientific and Technical English to Non-Native Speakers', *English Teaching Forum*, XV:2 (April 1977), 11–17 (a revised version of a paper written by Mary Todd Trimble and presented by her at the 4th International Congress of Applied Linguistics, Stuttgart, West Germany, August 1975); the published version was originally a lecture given by Louis Trimble at Sarajevo and at Skofja Loka, Yugoslavia, September 1975

Mary Todd Trimble and Louis Trimble, 'The Development of EFL Materials for Occupational English'; initially published in a shortened version in *English for*

Specific Purposes: An International Seminar, The British Council (Bogotá, Colombia), 1978, pp. 52–70; published in a complete version in *English for Specific Purposes: English for Science and Technology*, ed. Mary Todd Trimble, Louis Trimble and Karl Drobnic, Oregon State University Press, 1979, pp. 74–132; originally presented as a paper read at the British Council International Latin American Seminar on English for Specific Purposes, Paipa and Bogotá, Colombia, 17–22 April 1977

Larry Selinker, Mary Todd Trimble and Louis Trimble, 'Rhetorical Function Shifts in EST Discourse', *TESOL Quarterly*, September 1978, pp. 311–20

Mary Todd Trimble and Louis Trimble, 'The Properties of English for Specific Purposes', *Proceedings of the Primer Curso Introductorio Sobre Lenguas para Objetivos Específicos*, CILOE I, Universidad Autonima Metropolitana (Xochimilco, Mexico), 1980, pp. 77–112; originally a joint presentation as a two-day lecture-workshop series at CILOE I, 11–12 July 1979

Mary Todd Trimble and Louis Trimble, 'The Rhetoric of Language for Specific Purposes as a Model for a Description of Communication', *Fachsprache* (Vienna), Sonderheft I, Proceedings of the Second European Symposium on Languages for Special Purposes, Bielefeld, West Germany, 1981, pp. 219–235; originally presented as a paper read at the Second European Symposium on LSP, Bielefeld, West Germany, 24–6 September 1979

Mary Todd Trimble and Louis Trimble, 'Rhetorical–Grammatical Features of Scientific and Technical Texts as a Major Factor in Written ESP Communication', *Proceedings of the Third European Symposium on Languages for Special Purposes*: 'Pragmatics and LSP', The LSP Centre, UNESCO, ALSED LSP Network and Newsletter, The Copenhagen School of Economics, Copehagen, Denmark, 1982, pp. 199–216; originally presented as a paper read at the Third European Symposium on Languages for Special Purposes, Copenhagen, Denmark, 17–19 August 1981

Mary Todd Trimble and Louis Trimble, 'Article Use in Written EST Discourse', *Reading for Professional Purposes: Methods and Materials in Teaching Languages*, ed. A. K. Pugh and J. M. Ulijn, ACCO, Leuven, Belgium, 1985; originally presented as a paper read at the International Symposium on Reading for Professional Purposes in Native and Foreign Languages, 2–4 August 1982, Eindhoven University, Eindhoven, The Netherlands

Index

Index